Part-Time Lawyer, Full-Time Fisherman

Russ Orkin

PALMETTO
PUBLISHING
Charleston, SC
www.PalmettoPublishing.com

Part-Time Lawyer, Full-Time Fisherman
Copyright © 2023 by Russell D. Orkin

Hardcover ISBN: 9798822921795
Paperback ISBN: 9798822921801

Acknowledgements

It takes a village to facilitate the thought processes of a first-time book author and to develop them into a readable manuscript. First and foremost, a big thank you to Ruth Walkup, my former secretary of many years, who agreed to work with me on this project. She put a voice app on my iPhone and transcribed my often-incoherent ramblings into a readable text. Thanks also to Molly Fitzerald and Frontiers International, who handled the booking of fifty years of outdoor adventures, and provided me with the chronology of those trips for use in this book. My first three editors gave life and meaning to my written word. My sister, Judy Rosenthal, provided the background and fact-checking for the chapters on immigration from Europe and Early Years. My granddaughter, Molly Wyner, made subtle but relevant suggestions to the first several chapters. My daughter, Pam Hansen, did the overall check of the manuscript and was my go-to person on all matters relating to the book. Thanks also to my friends and neighbors, Al Ciocca and his wife, Patty, who made the final check of the manuscript before it was sent to the publisher, Palmetto Publishing, and my project manager, Anthony Ferrese. And finally, to my wife of sixty-three years, Sue, who once again tolerated my disruption of a normal lifestyle in favor of my latest adventure.

Cast of Characters

William Webb (deceased) – senior lawyer and mentor
Julius "Judy" Melvin Orkin (deceased) – father
Alice Elizabeth Golomb Orkin (deceased) – mother
Louis and Hermine Kahn Orkin (deceased) – paternal grandparents
Golombs (deceased) – maternal grandparents
Sue Scott Orkin – wife of sixty-three years
Mr. Mendelson – only survivor of Žagarė
Judy Orkin Rosenthal – sister
Fred Orkin – cousin
Sylvia Orkin – wife of Fred Orkin
Jim Drainer – employee of J.M. Orkin Excavating who bought the
    business
George Spencer (deceased) – friend of Russ's dad and Russ's boss at
    the furniture store
Dick Schafrath (deceased) – professional football player
Dave Love (deceased) – childhood friend
Dr. Morton "Mort" Rosenthal (deceased)– husband of Judy Orkin
    Rosenthal
Dr. Mike Klein (deceased) – friend of Mort
Dr. Marv Sobel (deceased) – friend of Mort
Sarge – college stadium dorm proctor
John McMahon – high school friend
Cam McMahon – high school and college friend, and best man
Dr. George St. Pierre – college professor

Steve Scott (deceased) – Sue's brother
Rabbi Jerome Folkman – marriage rabbi
Lee Asseo – sixty-plus year friend
Sheila Asseo (deceased) – wife of Lee Asseo
Dean Lee (deceased) – dean of John Marshall Law School
Paul Reznick – law partner
Richard "Rick" Byrne – law partner
Nathan "Nate" Prepelka – law partner
William "Bill" Logsdon (deceased) – law partner
Dee Murgi – law office receptionist
Bob "Demo" DeMajistre – former law partner, friend, and client
Dr. Suzuki (deceased) – Japanese lawyer, Tokyo
Brian Orkin – son
Jill Orkin Scott – daughter
Pam Orkin Hansen – daughter
Andy Hansen – son-in-law
Steve Mendelson – ex-son-in-law
Jess Peachey – client
Herman Myers (deceased) – client
Simon Bastacky - client
Alex Hrebeniuk – client
Bob Oglevee (deceased) – client
Mr. McConnell (deceased) – client
Mr. Bradley (deceased) – client
Berne Evans – client
Frank Calandra (deceased) – client
Frank Locotos – client
Mick Wilkes – client
George Tippins (deceased) – client
John Thomas – client
Alec Keith – client
Fritz van Langsdorf – German citizen
Emil Hermann (deceased) – Pittsburgh general practitioner
Wayne Alderson (deceased) – client

Nancy Alderson (deceased) – wife of Wayne Alderson
Nancy Jean McDonnell – daughter of Wayne Alderson
Stuart Meiklejohn – attorney
Herr Wolf – head of research for Lohmann
Brendon Byrne – witness for Seton
Mr. Matsui (deceased) – Japanese lawyer, Tokyo
Mr. Osamu Kitamura (deceased) – Japanese lawyer, Osaka
Mr. Im – Korean patent attorney, Seoul
Taka Kitaura – Japanese patent attorney and former Webb intern
Yoon Kim – Korean patent attorney and former Webb intern
Wilhelm Elsner (deceased) – European client
Andrea Ludwig – daughter of Wilhelm Elsner
Jule Tomar (deceased) – client from Haiti
Bill Hill – long-time friend
Freddie Smith – long-time friend
Bob Brasso - friend
John Shallenberger – long-time friend
Tad Potter (deceased) – long-time friend
Keith Helfer – long-time friend
Tip Davidson – sixty-plus year friend
Denny Lodge – friend
Buzzy Lodge (deceased) – friend
Don Lampus – friend and client
Phil Thomas – friend
Lou Kushner – long-time friend
Jack Demos – long-time friend
Denny Slevin – long-time friend
Beau Strathman – guide in the Bahamas and Missouri
Paul Hindes – Family Tyes® founder
Chuck McKinney – Family Tyes® founder
Dave Thorn – Family Tyes®
Bob Bergquest – guide on the Bighorn
Gordon Schmidt – long-time friend
Ed Watters – long-time friend

Charlie Isseroff – guide on Lake Mistassini

George Kelley – owner of King Fisher Lodge and guide on the Bighorn

John Green – guide – Spring Creeks, Montana

Amy and Jake – guides in Alaska

Table of Contents

Chapter I

Introduction

Gather a few lawyers, loosen them up with a beer or two, or other alcoholic beverages, and the stories start to fly. There are clients with unreasonable expectations. Clients who do not tell the entire truth to their lawyers. Clients who lie. Clients who are slow pay; clients who are no pay. Clients who think they know more than their lawyer. Crochety old judges who are difficult to work with. Verdicts or judgements that are either outlandish or are excessive, making the lawyer happy or unhappy depending on what side you are on. These stories continue unabated with the following limitation, that is the stories are limited by the Attorney-Client privilege, which maintains all clients' information as confidential and for which there is no statute of limitations. It allows for a full disclosure to the lawyer without fear that the information will be revealed to others. In Pennsylvania, the obligation exists under the Pennsylvania Code of Professional Conduct for Attorneys. This therefore puts certain limits on the scope and content of the stories that are being offered by the lawyers.

Now, gather a few fishermen and loosen them up with a few beers or other alcoholic beverages and the stories start to fly. There are no limitations on these stories. The first liar really does not have a chance. These stories include that fish were not biting; it was too hot; it was too cold; it was too calm; it was too rough; there was a full moon; there was a change in barometric pressure. As to the bonefish fishermen, it was too cloudy and you could not see the fish. As to the trout fishermen, the pH was wrong; the alkalinity was wrong; the oxygen content was wrong; the mayflies are late; the caddis flies are only hatching at night; the only fly on the water is the midge and, while the fisherman has midge flies, they are so small they cannot be seen to tie them on. The biggest story of all, which every fisherman tells, is about the big one that got away!

My story goes on with the lawyers' side being somewhat limited, but with the fishing side being wide open.

How did I arrive at the name for this book? It was easy. I left the steel industry and joined The Webb Law Firm in the spring of 1967. I had previously come to Pittsburgh for an interview. It was my first ever visit to the city. Sue and I decided that it was time for me to change careers, so we asked each other where we had the most fun. The answer was Columbus, Ohio, which is where I met Sue and where we both attended Ohio State University. With that established, Sue took my resume and sent it to a headhunter in Columbus. There it was obtained by the Webb firm in Pittsburgh, which at that time was known as Webb, Burden, Robinson and Webb. I later found out that I was not the Webb firm's first choice, but the practicing patent attorney from Westinghouse who received the job did not last long and, therefore, my name came to the top of the list. The Webb firm at the time was very small. I was the sixth lawyer and the eleventh employee. The foundation of the firm was built by Mr. William Webb, who became my mentor for the first many years I was with the firm. Mr. Webb was a very, very tough lawyer, and a perfect gentleman, kind, generous, and caring. About the third or fourth Christmas I was there, Mr. Webb threw his annual Christmas party in our conference room, and brought in food and beverages from the Duquesne Club. He presented me with a T-shirt that said "Part-time lawyer, full-time fisherman." That has stuck with me for many years, and is the source of the title of this book.

Remember the following little saying, origin of which is unknown. When the wind is from the east, fishing is least. When the wind is from the west, fishing is best. When the wind is from the south, the bait goes into the fish's mouth. When the wind is from the north, fishermen don't go forth.

I hope you enjoy the following stories as much as I enjoy bringing them to you.

Chapter II

Immigration from Europe

A. The Orkin Clan

My dad, Julius Melvin Orkin known as "Judy" by all his friends, was born December 2, 1900 in Brownhelm, Ohio. His parents, Louis Orkin and Hermine Kahn Orkin, came to this country through the Port of Baltimore from Eastern Europe in 1888 and settled in Baltimore. Hermine Kahn arrived in 1892 and married Louis. They moved to Brownhelm, where they started farming. After several years, they relocated to the Highland Farm in Unionville, Ohio, where they were tenant farmers.

There were ten brothers and sisters in the Orkin family and, in the early 1900's, they formed a corporation in the state of Ohio called "The Ten Tribes of Orkin," one for each sibling in the family. The preamble to the articles of incorporation tells it all.

> We, the members of "The Ten Tribes of Orkin," in order to strengthen the ties of relationship, maintain and preserve the unity of the family, ensure its tranquility, promote its welfare, elevate the educational, moral, and social standard of its members, assist each other and give charity to deserving members in distress, do ordain and establish this organization known as "The Ten Tribes of Orkin" which has been incorporated under the laws of the state of Ohio and having duly received its charter

from the Secretary of said state of Ohio, do adopt the following laws to wit.

We were able to locate a number of letters from the early 1920's, acknowledging receipt from organizations such as The Jewish Orphans of Poland, the War Orphans Bureau for the Joint Distribution Committee of the American Funds for Jewish War Sufferers and a number more.

Starting in the mid-1880's, about ninety Jewish immigrant families located in the Cleveland area. This was made possible through the generosity of Baron Maurice de Hirsch, a European financier. He was a humanitarian who was concerned about the fate of European Jews after the assassination of Czar Alexander II. He established a fund from which Jewish families could take out loans to purchase land in several preselected areas. The Baron envisioned a kibbutz-like community, which did not materialize.

The Louis Orkin family was the first, and they settled in a little community known as Unionville in northeastern Ohio. They purchased a small farm and then later moved to the Highland Farm, which was close by in the town of Geneva. They relocated to Geneva, Ohio and into a rambling house with a wonderful front porch. This house became a getaway for my aunts and uncles from the Cleveland area, who routinely came out to enjoy the country life and enjoy Geneva-on-the-Lake, a popular summer resort. From time to time, my grandmother housed foster Jewish children who were sent from Cleveland. My grandmother was the matriarch of the family and was an elegant lady who brought her impeccable style and manners to the farm. Legend has it that she never left the house without her hat and white gloves. She had empathy for the underprivileged and collected used clothing, which she then redistributed. She was highly principled and my favorite story which marks her place in the family is as follows.

Duke Ellington and his band were scheduled to play at the dance hall at Geneva-on-the-Lake in the early 1930's, but alas no one would rent to Blacks at that time, so they had no place to sleep. My grandmother hitched up her horse and buggy and called upon the mayor, where she voiced her disapproval and offered her farm for their use. It was a *fait accompli.*

Seven of her eight children left the Geneva area as they became young adults, and only my father remained in the area.

B. The Golomb Clan

My mom, Alice Elizabeth Golomb Orkin, was born in New York City in 1906. My maternal grandparents came from Vilnius, Lithuania. They basically spoke Yiddish and followed their familiar customs. My maternal grandparents became the largest grape farmers in northeastern Ohio; my grandmother, Rachael, was the business head of the farm and my grandfather, Joseph, was the farmer. Joseph had a very outgoing personality. He was a Tevye-like person who sang and danced at every gathering. He was very proud and liked everything to be the best. They built a beautiful brick home among all the little farmhouses. He furnished it with elegant pieces of furniture, and then went to buy a car, the first in Ashtabula County. He drove the car home but was unable to stop it and ended up driving it right through the garage door wall.

The Golomb and Orkin families were among the leaders in the community. They were officers of the Jewish Farmer Association, who produced sixty percent of the district's grape crop. Unfortunately, my grandfather lost everything in the Great Depression. They had a single customer, and supplied Welch's Foods Inc. with concord grapes. Therefore, when everybody went belly-up over the Depression, my grandfather was soon to follow. He spent his last couple of years living with my family in Geneva, and all I can remember is that he loved to put ketchup on his eggs and every Sunday night he would put his ear up to the radio and would listen to "The Lone Ranger."

In 2007, Sue and I, along with my sister Judy and my cousin Fred Orkin and his wife Sylvia, took an Orkin family "roots" tour to Russia, Latvia, Lithuania, and Estonia.

In Lithuania, we called upon the archivist in Vilnius, the capital, and learned that there had been a large population of Orkins in a little town called Žagarė, which is on the Latvia/Lithuania border. All the

Jewish population in that town had been killed by the Russians except for one sixteen-year-old boy who was conscripted into the Russian army. When he returned, he found that the entire Jewish population was gone. He was still alive in 2007 when we visited, and our tour guide knew him. His name was Mr. Mendelson. We visited him and he took us to the two Jewish cemeteries where all the Orkins are buried. It turns out that the day we visited was his eightieth birthday and his children from Russia could not come to visit him, so we threw him a Pittsburgh birthday party and we gave him a Pittsburgh Pirates baseball hat, a hundred dollars, and a wonderful dinner. I am sure he remembered his eightieth birthday for the rest of his life.

Now a little bit about my parents. My dad was quiet, thoughtful, dependable, and nonjudgmental; he was a pillar of the community. He was active politically, and was involved in city and county government. He conducted his life with dignity and had the highest moral standards. I never heard him raise his voice. I never heard him swear and I never heard him disparage anyone. He started his own business, J.M. Orkin Excavating and Trucking, by buying an International dump truck. He backed down to the beach at Geneva-on-the-Lake and loaded sand by hand, which he then sold to the townspeople. Eventually, he added a second dump truck, D-2 and D-4 Caterpillar tractors, a road grader, and a highway roller. He dug basements, installed septic tanks, and did the excavating for the various developers in the area.

He won fame as a pitcher in the Ohio, Pennsylvania, and New York areas. In the summer of 1928, he played for the Huntsburg Baseball Team, which won the Suburban League Championship along with the Geauga County Crown and the Ashtabula County title. His pitching record was amazing that year. He was the only pitcher on that team and so could never look to a bullpen and was required to pitch every game. In that season, he recorded twenty-seven victories without taking a loss. He started playing baseball in high school and, after he graduated in 1918, he embarked on a baseball career that continued until World War II. During those twenty years, he played with and against some of the best teams in the entire area. For a while, he pitched AAA ball in

Cleveland until the amateur officials discovered that he had played with the semi-pro Dunkirk, New York team. The highlight of his career was pitching against Satchel Page. He was courted by the major leagues, but my grandmother would not let him go, saying that was no job for a Jewish boy. He tried to join the US Army but was too old and they would not accept him so, during the war, he joined the Coast Guard Reserve, where he remained until the war's end.

An interesting story involves a trip I took. I was driving somewhere when I got picked up by the State Highway Patrol for speeding. The officer looked at my license and looked back at me and asked if I was any relation to Judy Orkin. I replied that he was my dad. For the next twenty minutes, he proceeded to wow me with stories about my dad's baseball prowess because he had played with him on the Dunkirk New York team. The conversation obviously ended without me getting a ticket and with me promising to tell my dad that his old teammate was okay.

My dad passed away far too young at age sixty-one. Visitation was held in the Belding Funeral Home in Geneva. I had never seen so many people lined up to pay their respects. There were as many people in overalls and work boots as there were people in suits and ties. He was truly a man of the people and he set a wonderful example, which I have tried to follow throughout my lifetime.

It is impossible to describe my mother in a few sentences. She was dynamic, she was very smart, very affectionate, and lots of fun. She was quick to react but quick to forget. She had strong leadership skills and was president of every civic organization in the Geneva, Ohio area. After my dad died, she continued to run his excavating business for a few years. Eventually, she tired of that and sold the business to Jim Drainer, who was the sole employee of the company and the bulldozer driver. In 1965, my mother then joined VISTA, Volunteers In Service To America, a program conceived by President Kennedy and instituted by President Johnson. She was trained at Hull House in Chicago, and soon thought of herself as the reincarnation of Jane Adams. This experience placed her among the poor and elderly in the slums of both Chicago and later in Miami, where the Cuban and Puerto Rican refugees were migrating into the country. Upon her retirement, she moved to Cleveland and worked with the elderly and the Russian immigrants for both Jewish Family Services and the JCC Nutrition Program. From her childhood, she was fluent in reading, writing, and speaking Yiddish, and she often spoke before a couple hundred immigrants, giving them directions on where they could obtain their social services and the like. She became the television spokesperson for VISTA, and I would get telephone calls from my friends at all strange hours of the day and night, saying that they had just seen my mother on TV. As a true grandmother to my children, they could do no wrong in her eyes and she was their advocate regardless of the circumstances.

Chapter III

Early Years

The first couple of years of my life were spent at the small home my dad had built on a one-acre plot that my grandmother had given him. We later moved to East Main Street in Geneva, just within the city limits. This ensured that I would attend the Geneva Area School systems for Grades 1-12. School was school, and I was a good student, taking college-preparatory courses as I got into the senior high school. From early on, I sensed that I would have to pay my own way through college and so, in the sixth grade, I got my first paper route, which I maintained for a year or so. I then went to work for George Spencer, who was a good friend of my dad's, and who owned the "Your Furniture Store." I worked after school and sports virtually every day of the week and all day on Saturday. I did this all the way through the twelfth grade, see Appendix I. When I turned sixteen and got my driver's license, I was able to drive the furniture van and deliver furniture, which I thoroughly enjoyed. Those were the days before queen- and king-sized mattresses, and I could deliver the full-sized mattresses without any assistance. On occasion, I would have to climb on top of the van with the mattresses to put them through the upstairs window when that was the only way to get to the second floor. Mr. Spencer was a very creative guy and he had me selling mattresses at the Ashtabula County Fair one year, which was a hoot!

We did not have television and evenings were spent playing cards with my dad or reading books from the library. On the card playing, my dad and I played cribbage two or three times a week; on weekends I played pinochle with the neighbors. I became skilled at cards and that worked to my advantage a great portion of my life as I became quite a bridge fanatic in college and then in my later years. Starting in the first grade, my mother would take my hand and we would walk a mile into town to the library. I later learned I was afraid of the librarian for several years. There never was a time when the house was not full of books and I became an avid reader early on.

Although I was very busy with school and work, I always found time for sports, where I still have a great interest. In junior high and high school, I played football, basketball, and baseball, and lettered in all three at Geneva High School. I also won the town tennis championship, which was no big deal since there were only a few tennis players in the area.

I was a very good baseball player, but not at the level of my dad. In football, I was just an average player, although in my senior year, I became a halfway decent center and middle linebacker. I remember playing an exhibition game before my senior year against Wooster High School. At that time, Wooster had a fullback named Dick Schafrath, who went on to be an All-American end at Ohio State and an All-Pro tackle for the Cleveland Browns. What I remember about the game is that he ran the ball up the middle every play and, being the middle linebacker, I got run over every play. Most of the time, his legs would get tangled with mine and he would fall after a very good gain. Football was not to be my career.

I was a much better basketball player and made honorable mention on the all-league team. I received a partial scholarship to Case Institute of Technology, which is now Case Western. Unfortunately, the amount of money it would cost in addition to the partial scholarship was more than I had, and therefore I had to pass up the basketball scholarship and go on to Ohio State, where it was more economically feasible.

Growing up in a small town with only a few Jewish families, I knew no anti-Semitism and probably did not know what the word even meant. One of my best friends was Dave Love, a kid from one of only a few black families. We often ate at each other's homes and I attended church with him on a few occasions. He was the punter on the football team and I was the center. In a very tight game, we had to punt from our twenty-five-yard line. Dave tended to stutter a little when he was nervous. He called out the signals, stuttering all the way, and it sort of sounded like "hu-hu-hut one, hu-hu-hut two," etc. I was laughing so hard, I centered it into the end zone and the other team fell on it for a touchdown. Our coach called me over and said that I had centered the ball further than our quarterback could pass it. As mentioned before, football was not to be my career. At our 1965 tenth class reunion, I was visiting my parents' grave site and Dave Love was also at the cemetery doing the same thing. He came over to talk to me and saw the Star of David on the tombstone. He said to me, "I never knew you were Jewish!" I said to him, "I always knew you were Black!" When Dave passed away in Boulder, Colorado, his family brought him home and buried him in the Geneva cemetery. The family asked me to do the eulogy and I considered that to be an honor.

All through my school years, I was an avid fisherman. It started when I was a youngster and would ride my bike down Austin Road, a dirt road between Geneva and Geneva-on-the-Lake. Along that route was an old farm owned by Mr. Blum, who my dad knew and who had a wonderful pond set off from the road. The pond was filled with panfish, bullheads, and carp. I would ride my bike there frequently with two or three hooks in my pocket and some fishing line and would cut a long branch off a tree and attach the line to the end and put the hook on. There was an old manure pile behind the barn at this farm and it was loaded with red worms. There was a pitchfork there and one scoop of the pitchfork and you would have a whole can full of little red worms. They were ideal for catching the panfish that were there as well as the bullheads. I never did catch a carp, but I never quit trying. As I got into junior high school, I became a meat fisherman 100%. In the spring, summer, and early fall, we relied on Lake Erie blue pike as part of the sustenance for our family. The Lake Erie blue pike is a tremendously good eating fish, part of the walleye family and Lake Erie was filled with them. Two or three times a week, my dad and I would go down to the lake, rent a small boat with a six-horsepower Elgin motor, and go out on the lake before dark. We would bring a lantern, put the lantern over the side of the boat to attract and catch minnows before heading out another quarter mile or so and catch our fill of Lake Erie blue pike. We spent several years sustaining ourselves on these fish. This is my favorite blue pike story. One evening my dad and I went to Lake Erie where we were going to rent a boat, but a storm had come up and it was very choppy and we were afraid to venture out. There was an old-timer at the boathouse who told my dad that he had a trot line just off shore and if we would go out in his boat to the trot line, he would get us a bunch of Lake Erie blue pike to take home for our dinner. I guess my dad thought twice about it, but we ended up doing it and unfortunately got caught in a huge storm. Lake Erie is known for its rough water because it is the shallowest of the Great Lakes. We got tossed around, the rain showers came, the lantern went out, we were hanging on for dear life, and ultimately, we were able to beach the boat about one mile from where the boat house was. I later learned that the old-timer was inebriated and neither of us recognized it before starting on our little adventure.

The sad end of this story is that the Lake Erie blue pike became extinct around 1962. The extinction was blamed on massive habitat loss including industrial waste, draining of wet lands, shoreline armoring, channelization of waterways, and extensive dredging along the harbors and shoreline of the Lake. Also at that time, there were high levels of phosphorus in the Lake. Bottom line, the end of the blue pike era.

I can only remember my mom and dad taking one vacation during this time period. They went to Florida for one week during my senior year. However, they both saw to it that my dad and I would go fishing in Canada every year. We drove to North Bay, Ontario, and the shores of Lake Nipissing. My dad's friend and my boss George Spencer and his son went with us on a couple of occasions, and later my brother-in-law, Dr. Mort Rosenthal, and his friends joined us. At North Bay, we boarded the Chief Commanda ferry boat and went across Lake Nipissing into the French River, where we stayed at the Keystone Fishing Lodge for a week.

The French River was loaded with walleyes and northern pike and an occasional muskie or two. On one occasion, we hooked a sturgeon, but were not able to land it. The fishing guides were Ojibwe Indians and there were shore lunches every day consisting of fried walleye and fried potatoes cooked in a pound of lard over an open fire. It was the best.

Mort and two of his doctor buddies, Mike Klein and Marv Sobel, from Mount Sinai Hospital in Cleveland went with us on a couple of occasions. They were rookies when it came to fishing, but they loved it dearly. I do remember one incident as we were traveling across Lake Nipissing on the Chief Commanda. There was an old guy full of whiskers and white hair, and he convinced my brother-in-law and the other two doctors to invest in his mining company called Beaucage Mine. I remember these three doctors pulling out their checkbooks and writing this old guy a check. I do not think they ever heard anything from Beaucage Mine, but I am sure they thought the trip was worth it because the fishing that followed was always delightful.

Chapter IV

College Days at Ohio State University

A. First Year

I had saved one thousand one hundred dollars over the previous six years of working at the furniture store, and was prepared to head off to college. I chose Ohio State because it was a large school and one that I could at least afford the first year. I had been to the campus a couple of times since our high school football team had been invited to attend an Ohio State football game almost each year. My favorite subjects were chemistry and math, so engineering was the obvious choice. I chose the cheapest housing, which happened to be the Ohio State stadium dormitory.

My dad and my uncle took me and my small metal foot locker to Columbus and to the famous Horseshoe Stadium. My room was on the top floor of a four-floor dormitory built inside of the stadium. It consisted of eighteen metal bunk beds, with each bunk bed having two metal standup lockers. In other words, there were thirty-six people in my room my freshman year. I happened to have the best dormitory room because there was a big window-like opening facing one end of the stadium, so I had a perfect view of the field from my bunk.

The room proctor was an older man we called Sarge, who was going to school on the GI Bill, and had been a former drill sergeant in the Marines. He was clearly the smallest person in the room, but we were all scared to death of him and he ruled the roost with an iron fist. We listened to him and he made sure we all studied and did all the things we were supposed to do as young freshmen.

My classes were interesting for the most part, and my high school education had been very helpful in the area of math and science thanks to very good teachers. In high school I was used to getting all A's with a rare B now and then. This continued my freshman year except for Engineering Drawing, in which I received a failing grade. I had trouble envisioning things in three dimensions. I immediately repeated and passed the course. It is interesting because later in life, as an intellectual property lawyer, I routinely dealt with various types of drawings and over time I finally got accustomed to working with them.

The highlight of my freshman year was the trip to Michigan for the Ohio State-Michigan football game in the fall of 1955. The train carrying the team and student body who elected to travel to the game left from the stadium. The cost was seventeen dollars per person, and I splurged since I was a big football fan. I went with my bunkmate, who was from North Canton, whose name unfortunately I cannot remember. He dropped out of school after the freshman year and, as I just cannot recall his name, I will simply refer to him as my bunkmate. The train left late in the evening or early in the morning, arriving well in advance of game time. It was a very snowy day, and snow fell throughout the game. Ohio State had a running back named Howard "Hopalong" Cassady, who was an All American, and this was going to be his last regular season game. We did all the foolish things young freshmen do including drinking beer on the train and using a hypodermic needle to fill oranges full of vodka, which we then consumed during the game. The game was very exciting, and Ohio State ultimately pulled out the victory. At the conclusion of the game, the Ohio State students ran out onto the field to tear down the goal post, which was the custom-ary thing to do at the Ohio State-Michigan games. Unfortunately, the Michigan student body surrounded the goal post and fought us tooth and nail and prevented us from getting to the goal post. I personally must have been knocked down five times, but continued to attempt to get there, which was totally unsuccessful. Everybody left the stadium including my bunkmate and me. I said to my bunkmate as we were outside, "Let's go get the goal post!" We then went to a gas station and bought a hacksaw, and we returned into the stadium. It was empty but for the press box, which was absolutely loaded with writers from all over the country. In those days, the writers remained in the press box and wrote their stories so, while the lights were still on in the stadium, everybody in the Press Corps. saw these two young guys take off their coats and shimmy up the goal post with the hacksaw. We then proceeded to cut down one of the uprights and removed it from the stadium. It was a very thick metal pipe and it was extremely heavy. Somehow, we were able to hide it at a factory adjacent the railroad track. We then went into town. By then, word had gotten around that someone had gotten the goal post and all the writers in the press box were writing stories about it. After the team showered and had some time to relax, everybody gathered at the train to board for the return trip back to Columbus. It was then that my bunkmate and I marched up with this heavy ten-foot pipe section on our shoulders with everyone applauding. We were greeted at the train by head coach Woody Hayes himself, who said we had done a wonderful job and requested that we give him the goal post and that he would cut it into five equal pieces. He said he had use for three of the pieces, and my bunkmate and I would each get a piece for our efforts and as our trophy. Since we lived in the stadium, it was very easy to pick up our large section of goal post, which I did. I took it home with me at the end of the school year. As the second year approached, I was getting ready to go back to school and my mother said to me that she had been cleaning out the basement and found an old piece of pipe, and so she threw it out. That was the bad news in my "good-news-bad-news" story of my claim to fame, namely, getting the goal post after an Ohio State victory at Michigan.

B. Second Through Fifth Years

I finished my freshman year at a cost of seven hundred dollars, leaving me four hundred dollars for the start of my sophomore year. I therefore had to find adequate employment to supplement my income. My dad got me a job at the Geneva Rubber Co., where I worked the midnight shift. It was piecework, so I got paid by what I produced. We made rubber parts and I ran the mold in the manufacturing process. The process was very difficult because there was a vertically movable table in front of a very large press. I could hydraulically move the table up and down, and I could manually move the mold into the press. The problem was that the mold weighed on the order of fifteen hundred pounds and therefore it was necessary to put a soap-like substance on the table so that the mold would slide easily off the table into the press. There was a block-and-tackle above the table so that when the mold came out of the press, I would attach the block-and-tackle to the top half of the mold and remove it, thereby exposing the rubber parts which were then removed with an air hose. It was then necessary to place rubber pieces in the mold and reverse the process, putting it again in the press for the next time. The problem was that in order to make money, you had to be very, very efficient, but if you tried to pull the mold too early, the rubber was not adequately cured and it was very difficult to remove the parts from the mold interior.

Working midnight to eight o'clock in the morning was also very difficult because it precluded me from doing the things I normally would do in the evenings. During the day, I often helped my dad in his business by driving a dump truck or doing other miscellaneous tasks, generally with a shovel. When I returned to school, I had adequate money for my second year. I upgraded and moved into Baker Hall, a much nicer dorm than the stadium. I had one roommate, and we lived on the J wing of Baker Hall. During my second year, I pledged a fraternity, ZBT, where my cousin happened to be President. However, I was not cut out for the fraternity life and did not have the money to have the proper clothing and the like. Therefore, I did not go ahead with my pledge in that fraternity and returned to the dormitory, where I worked on setting up a social group on the J wing. We called the social group Jello and, for the next three years, Jello was a very important part of the social life for myself and all the others in the dormitory.

During my sophomore year, I chose metallurgical engineering as my major. There was money available in a scholarship fund sponsored by the American Foundry Society (AFS) and I applied for and obtained three hundred dollars per year. I eventually became President of the student chapter of the AFS and The American Institute for Metallurgical Engineering. Once established as a lawyer, I repaid my scholarship many times over through contributions to AFS.

Between my sophomore and junior years, I got a job at the Electro-metallurgical Plant (Electro-Met) in Ashtabula, OH. This too proved to be a very difficult job. The plant manufactured calcium carbide from lime and coke in an electric furnace at 3990°F. The product was then crushed and put in hoppers along a manufacturing line. The operator released the product from the hopper into a drum capable of holding one hundred pounds of material. The drum was sitting on a vibrating table and the product was forced into the drum with the benefit of a funnel and short wooden staff. About the time you finished packing the drum, the light on the hopper would go on, indicating that the next one-hundred-pound lot was in the hopper and ready for packing. This went on continuously for the entire eight-hour shift. Water and calcium carbide form acetylene gas. Therefore, if your entire body was not covered and if you were sweating, the dust from the operation would settle on your skin and combine with the moisture and burn your skin through the formation of acetylene gas. Many days, I ended up having to go to the infirmary before going to work to get the exposed parts of my body taped so that I would not get additional burns.

I alternated between second and third shift so, again, my days were left for sleeping and helping my dad in his excavating business.

My first inkling that I was going to be a lawyer occurred on that particular job. I was working the four to midnight shift on a Friday night and I had a date that I was to meet at a beach party after work. Thinking about it, I got a little excited and asked one of my buddies on the operating line to check me out at the end of the shift by putting my card through the checkout machine. I left about a half hour early and headed for the beach.

When I arrived to work on Monday morning, my card was not where it belonged and there was a note to see the general foreman. I went into the general foreman's office and he informed me that he knew that I had left early and that I was subject to being fired. It was then that I used every verbal skill I had to convince him to give me another chance, because the thought of having to tell my dad that I had gotten fired for some stupid thing like leaving early because I had a date was more than I could handle. The general foreman was understanding and gave me a second chance, and I toed the line and became the model employee for the rest of the summer.

My third year at school went smoothly and I was near the top of my class. There were two extremely bright students ahead of me and I was never able to catch them academically. I did drive out to the Rose Bowl with two brothers (John and Cam McMahon) from Geneva in 1957. We drove straight through with one stop from Ashtabula County in northeast Ohio to Pasadena, where we stayed with relatives of the brothers.

The father of the McMahon brothers managed a bar at the summer resort at Geneva-on-the-Lake, and he let us use his car. The owner of the bar was a high-flying entrepreneur who spent the winter in Las Vegas. When he learned we were driving to Los Angeles, he told us to stop at the Golden Nugget, where he would be, so he could say hello and welcome us to Las Vegas. We made that stop and found the owner sitting at a poker table in the middle of a big poker game. He excused himself and went to this huge restroom area, where he proceeded to get a shave as he lectured us on the ifs, ands, and buts of Las Vegas. He then gave each of us a twenty-five-dollar chip for use at the Golden Nugget. When we started the trip, I had the most money of the three of us, seventy-two dollars. The other two each had on the order of fifty dollars. Therefore, we were suddenly each given another twenty-five dollars, with the choice being to either keep it and add it to our spending money or simply blow it, which the owner had intended us to do. John elected to cash in the twenty-five-dollar chip and he proceeded to lose it in about thirty minutes. I thought long and hard. I cashed in the chip, put half of it in my wallet and blew the other half. Cam cashed the chip and put all the money in his wallet. Later in life, John turned out to be a tax collector for the state of Ohio; I had a pretty good career; and my buddy Cam, who saved all the twenty-five dollars, became President of Shell Oil Pipeline. Cam was also the best man in my wedding.

We whooped and hollered in Pasadena, and spent New Year's Eve at the famous Coconut Grove nightclub in the Ambassador Hotel on Wilshire Boulevard where Guy Lombardo led the New Year's Eve band.

Following my third year, I got a job as a state inspector on Route 90, which was under construction in northern Ohio. My boss knew I needed money to attend school so, in addition to working days, he often let me work the midnight shift as well. My primary responsibility was to check that all the drainage lines and catch basins were put in properly. For this I had a small transit, in which I would check to see that the trenches had the proper slope and that they were filled with the proper amount of stone prior to the trenches being filled. It was on that job that I learned a very important lesson in life. Every few miles, there were bridges over the highway being constructed. I was checking the blueprints when I noticed that the construction company had failed to put a crossover in underneath one of the bridges. The construction company was a very large highway company called S.J. Grove out of Michigan. I called this oversight to the General Foreman's attention and he said that they had difficulty because they could not get their big equipment underneath the bridge to dig the crossover. I was not buying this so he left in his pickup truck. About an hour later he showed up and rolled down the window. When I walked over to the truck, he took a roll of twenty-dollar bills and reached out the window and handed it to me. My first impulse was to lift my arm to take the money because I sorely needed money, and then I realized what was going on and I glared at him. I told him to go get a labor crew and dig it by hand and I fully expected that crossover to be done properly, which he ultimately did.

My fourth year at school also went smoothly, and I continued to have more than adequate grades. I was still living in Baker Hall in the J wing. We won the intramural softball championship and came in second in the intramural basketball program for the entire university. This was made possible because, as part of our group, we had Bobby Knight and John Havlicek (two of the more famous OSU athletes from that era) and they got some of their jock buddies to play on our teams with us so we were virtually unbeatable.

Between my fourth and fifth years, I reached the age of twenty-one and I worked as the daytime bartender at The Barn, which was one of the top entertainment facilities at Geneva-on-the-Lake. My boss was Mr. McMahon, the father of John and Cam, with whom I went to California. I opened the bar at eight o'clock in the morning and worked until four thirty in the afternoon, when I was relieved by the evening and night crews. Again, because I needed to make money, I often came back and waited tables in the evening for additional income. The bar was located across from the burlesque theater. The burlesque theater was famous for having the top-name burlesque queens throughout the course of the summer. Every morning as I would open the bar, there would be a line of burlesque girls from across the street waiting to get to the bar. Each one had a different story about the mean comedians and what went wrong the previous night. I felt like I should have changed my career from engineering to sociology or psychology since each girl would come to me with their sad tale of woe and I would have to comfort them and advise them on the steps to take to keep the comedians from being mean to them and the like. It was quite an experience for a summer job.

My fifth year was very interesting. I moved into a house with four of my friends. Every year, a fifth-year student got picked by the graduate school to work in the lab as a lab assistant. A great debate went on between the two young men who were first and second in the school of metallurgical engineering as to which one would get picked for the job. I assured them that was not the case and that I would end up getting picked. When I got picked, they both approached me and asked how I knew I was going to be picked. I said the graduate students needed a fourth for bridge and I was the best bridge player among the group. Anybody could clean test tubes and light Bunsen burners. They were more interested in finding a good fourth for bridge than they were for some genius to clean out the test tubes. That expertise in bridge has carried through to the present.

During my fifth year, the entire senior class took a week trip to Chicago to visit a number of metal-producing companies. The trip leader and our chaperone was Dr. George St. Pierre, a young, well-liked professor, who taught physical chemistry and other high-level courses. George's favorite pastime was playing bridge with his wife as partner, so you know where I spent my evenings. Dr. St. Pierre became one of the expert witnesses in the Basic Oxygen Steel litigation being handled by The Webb Law Firm, where I spent fifty-four years of my adult life. It was most enjoyable to again spend time with Dr. St. Pierre.

Chapter V

Wedding Bells

Sometime during my fourth year at Ohio State, I had a blind date with Sue Scott, who was from Wellston, Ohio. We dated throughout my fourth and fifth years at school. When it appeared that we were getting serious, she invited me to her home in Wellston, Ohio. Wellston is a small town in the middle of Appalachia. I was a little apprehensive about going to southern Ohio for this trip, but agreed to do so. The roads in southern Ohio are quite hilly, and there was not a whole lot of things happening in Appalachia that I was familiar with. We drove to Wellston that day with friends of hers from Wellston who were going home for the weekend. We were traveling on Route 327, which is a hilly, two-lane road in the middle of nowhere. As we were traveling further and further into the hills, I wondered how I got myself into this to begin with. We suddenly approached a little town called Ray, Ohio. There was an old rickety house with a swing on the front porch, and an old couple sitting on the porch swinging. I had never seen anything quite like that in my life. They pulled in front of that house and Sue said, "Mom and Dad are waiting for us." I immediately started trying to think where a bus station might be so that I could get a bus back to Columbus. As I got out of the car and started to open my trunk to get my suitcase, the other couple and Sue broke out laughing. They had set me up for this and it worked, much to my chagrin.

Anyway, back into the car we went and drove to Sue's home in Wellston. It was a very nice home on a hill across the street from her grandfather's slaughter house, which her dad was running along with one of his brothers. Sue's brother Steve took me over to see her grandfather at the slaughterhouse. He was sitting in a rocking chair with a mean-looking Dalmatian underneath him. Steve said, "Grandpa, I'd like you to meet Sue's friend, Russ." Grandpa, who was hard of hearing, said, "Gus, it's very nice to meet you." From that day forward, Steve called me Gus and we always got a laugh out of that.

Sometime after graduation, I gave Sue an engagement ring, and the wedding was set for New Year's Eve 1960. I had left for my job at Inland Steel in June of 1960. I had an old 1953 Plymouth that was about to fall apart so, with my first paycheck, I purchased a 1960 Triumph TR3. It was a beautiful car, a British racing green with a beige top and a black hardtop for winter. Sue remained in Columbus for the fall of 1960 getting ready for the wedding. Sue was a good Methodist at that time, but somehow my mom had convinced her that she ought to attend lessons in Judaism so she knew what she was getting into. This was rather surprising since I had never had any training in the Jewish religion and have not to this day. As winter approached, I had to return to Columbus for my blood test, which was required prior to the wedding. I got into my TR3 and started toward Columbus, when I burned out the clutch. Therefore, I had to take the car to a dealer to have it repaired, and I jumped on a train to Columbus. When I got to Columbus, Steve picked me up and we went off to get the bloodwork done. When the nurse stuck me to draw the blood, I immediately passed out. To this day, Sue said that was probably a message that I failed to appreciate.

Our wedding night was a white-out snow storm in Columbus, Ohio. The service was performed by Rabbi Jerome Folkman, with whom Sue had been taking classes. The wedding was at Temple Israel, located on the east end of Columbus. The wedding was a wonderful affair, and both of our parents were able to attend. My dad had had a stroke and died in March of 1961, so it was a blessing that he was able to attend the wedding.

Our wedding night was spent in a hotel in Columbus. Sue claims that, on our wedding night, I watched an Ohio State basketball game because Ohio State was on its way to winning the NCAA championship. I had to admit that I did watch some of the game but I wanted to remind her what a wonderful halftime we had, details of which I will keep to myself.

Sunday morning, after our first night of marital bliss, we headed to Chicago because I had to start work on Monday in the steel mill. The trip to Chicago was anything but enjoyable because there was no heater in the car and both Sue and I were freezing as we drove. We stopped in Marysville, Ohio at a restaurant called Dilly's Dump and had breakfast, and then we drove to Munster, Indiana, where we rented a townhouse under the Tristate Expressway.

While Sue's parents lived in Wellston, we made numerous trips there. Her aunts, uncles, and cousins were wonderful friendly people, and we spent many a night playing penny ante poker and/or euchre. The very first Christmas after our wedding, we were planning to go to Wellston, leaving late Friday afternoon after work. Sue by then was also working as a secretary to the dean of a small college in Harvey, Illinois. It was snowing, so I said that we had to wait until the next day because the TR3 was not good in snow. Sue laid on the bed and kicked her feet in anger and frustration, so we of course left in the snow storm. I drove and as we got off the turnpike outside of Toledo to head south to the hills, I got picked up by a police officer in a small town for speeding. I told the police officer that I was on my way to my wife's home for Christmas and I knew I was going a little fast, but I was tired and about to turn the driving over to my wife. He bought this so I told Sue to quickly slide over and start driving before he changed his mind. The problem was the center console and gear shift were in the way and she did not have room to slide over. She eventually made it and I told her to get the heck going. The seat was back and she could not reach the clutch pedal. She proceeded to start and stop in quick jerks, causing her to peal rubber over and over. I think the police officer was happy to get us out of his town so he let us be on our merry way to Wellston for Christmas.

There are a couple of fishing stories in connection with the first year of our marriage. In the summer of 1961, we went with Judy and Mort to Georgian Bay to do some fishing. Georgian Bay can be quite rough, and we were in a boat rocking and rolling with the waves as were trying to fish. It got very rough and everybody was hanging on as we made our way back to shore. When we got there, Sue, with her wonderful Scotch-Irish temper, said that both she and Judy were almost falling out of the boat and when they looked at Mort and me, we were hanging on to our rods and tackle boxes so that they would not go overboard. At that point, Sue declared that she never wanted to go fishing with me again for the rest of our lives and, for the next sixty-three years with a few exceptions, I have tried to live up to that role that she identified for me.

One exception was the next summer, we again went on a fishing trip with Mort and Judy, this time to Hayward, Wisconsin, the muskie capital of the world. It was proper to use a motor to navigate the boat, but it was illegal to troll for muskie, and I had to row the boat while Mort cast unsuccessfully for muskie all over the lake. Meanwhile, the girls were back in the cabin chatting about whatever. After rowing for about six hours, I was tired and I told Mort that I was going back to camp to visit with the girls and he could go out by himself if he wanted to keep fishing. He dropped me off, started the motor, and took off for the middle of the lake, where he was going to do some additional fishing. About an hour later, he showed up at our cabin with a towel over his hand. He removed the towel and a treble hook from a Jointed Pikie Minnow had gone all the way through his finger and was coming out the other end. He was a wonderful physician but, since he was the one in trouble, there was not a lot he could do. Judy, who spent a lifetime in nursing and managing nurses, immediately gave him a bottle of whiskey and we headed for town to have the Jointed Pikie removed from his finger. We got to a doctor's office and the doctor immediately agreed to see him. Mort was in the doctor's office a great deal longer than we thought he would be and we could not figure out why. When he came out, he had a wonderful grin on his face and the doctor was with him, arm in arm. It turned out that the doctor had been in World War II as a physician, very close to where Mort had been in World War II, so they became bosom buddies and Mort was particularly happy because he tended to be a little on the thrifty side and the doctor had given him professional courtesy and removed the fish hook at no charge.

Chapter VI

Steel Mill Days

During my fifth year at Ohio State, I was offered two permanent positions following graduation. One was with Union Carbide in Alloy, West Virginia and the other with Inland Steel in East Chicago, Indiana with the headquarters being in downtown Chicago. It was not much of a decision for a twenty-two-year-old and I readily accepted the job at Inland Steel.

Following graduation, I headed back to Geneva-on-the-Lake and my bartending job for a month or so, and then I left for the big city of Chicago and my career as a metallurgical engineer. I roomed at Mrs. Loftus's boarding house for eight dollars per week. The other boarder was Lee Asseo, who turned out to be one of my best friends for the rest of my life. He was only there for the summer because he was on an Inland Steel scholarship from Cornell University, where he was in his fifth year. He only paid seven dollars per week, but that was because he had a smaller closet than I did.

My starting salary was five hundred thirty dollars per month, which I thought was incredible at that time. I was hired by the quality control department and started work in the spring of 1960.

After a short indoctrination, I became the metallurgist at Number 2 cold mill. The cold mill consisted of multiple pickling lines, four high tandem mills, annealing furnaces, temper mills, and various other finishing equipment to make coils or sheets of steel. I had a crew of about twenty-five inspectors, three foremen, and a clerk.

Later, when I became a lawyer, I represented many steel manufacturing companies and many steel equipment supply companies. It included Tippins Machine, which developed new rolling mills and improved ways of transforming steel slabs into steel coils. My experience from my cold mills days at Inland Steel proved to be invaluable as I represented Tippins Machine and other companies in the steelmaking business.

After about two and a half years in the cold mill, I was promoted to the supervising metallurgist in the tin mill. Interestingly, there were only three primary customers for tin plate, namely American Can Company, Continental Can Company, and Crown Cork & Seal Company Inc., all of which were in the Chicago area.

I had a small crew who continually checked the quality of the tin plate being produced. Our service rep routinely called on these three customers. I would accompany him when there were quality issues to address. Every meeting with one of these three can companies started with a very short inspection of the quality problems that had been encountered. This short inspection was followed by an extremely long lunch, during which the can company purchasing agent and the Inland service rep partook of multiple martinis and discussed everything except the quality problem we were there to discuss. I would join them for one but had to be careful since I had to then drive home from Chicago or head into law school, which I had started in the spring of 1961.

After a one-year stay in the tin mill, I was promoted to supervising metallurgist in steelmaking. This was a very responsible position. Inland was the single largest steel mill plant in the United States. There were three open-hearth shops with a total of thirty-seven open-hearth furnaces. During my tenure there, we tested basic oxygen furnace (BOF) steel slabs from McLouth Steel and thereafter added the first of two BOF steel-making furnaces. Steelmaking was changed from heats of steel made during eight hours of cooking in an open-hearth furnace to heats of steel made in thirty minutes in a BOF vessel. This tremendous advance in technology was first developed by the Austrian government using injection nozzles that injected oxygen beneath the surface of the steel to oxidize the impurities and refine the steel. This technology was licensed in the United States by the Austrian government through Kaiser Steel in California. Our law firm represented the Austrian Government and Kaiser in a series of BOF litigations that were just finishing up when I joined the firm in the spring of 1967.

I had responsibility for around-the-clock open-hearth inspectors, who continuously sampled the steel being made for chemical analysis and then observed after the furnace was tapped into a huge ladle, the pouring of the steel from the ladle into ingot molds pulled by a train along a pouring platform. In addition to the open-hearth inspectors, I was responsible for inspectors in the blooming and slabbing mills, where the ingots of steel were transformed into product for further processing. The interesting thing about the inspectors in the blooming and slabbing mills is that they were mostly older women who were still there from the World War II days when they were the only ones available to work in the mills. These women were my best inspectors, but scheduling them was a real pain, because of their many marital problems and their preferences of what shift they wanted to work, etc.

I met once a week with the operating people in each open-hearth shop, where I went over the quality issues that had arisen over the previous week. Most of these issues involved making the required chemistries in the open-hearth shops and the surface quality of the slabs being produced in the slabbing and blooming mills.

When I left Inland Steel for The Webb Law Firm in the spring of 1967, I had spent three and a half years as the chief metallurgist of steelmaking.

My extracurricular activities were limited since I was attending law school as well as working at the mill. In my last position as the metallurgist of steelmaking, I had twenty-four-hour responsibility at the mill and if there were heats of steel and the like that had not met the chemistry or other quality requirements, I was occasionally called out to the mill at all hours to deal with the problem of converting the steel to other orders and applications that were not originally scheduled. This became very challenging since all the time I was the metallurgist for steelmaking, I was also in law school. It was very difficult and tiring to spend all day in the mill, go to law school, and then return to the mill for these additional problems that occurred from time to time.

I had no time for extracurricular activities, but I did manage to play a little bridge at lunchtime and enjoy a fishing trip or two during this time period. The practice foreman at Number 3 open-hearth was a big fisherman and he and I would occasionally take off on a Saturday and go to southern Indiana and fish in some of the local lakes in that part of the country. I always got a kick out of his technique, which was to take binoculars and, when we got on these little lakes, he would scout the other boats and attempt to find farmers in overalls because he figured they knew what they were doing and we did not, so we would merely go fish near the boats where there were farmers having their recreational fling.

During these seven years in the steel mill, I learned a couple of very important lessons that helped me throughout my career as a lawyer. Whether I was in the cold mill, tin mill, or steelmaking operation, there were always conflicts between the operating people who were interested in production, the quality control people who were interested in maintaining the quality of steel, and the sales department who were responsible for satisfying the customer. Over the years, there were many conflicts between these three entities. In every single conflict, the sales department was the victor. It taught me that meeting customer requirements was always the primary goal and, for this reason, the sales department won every single dispute over the operating people and the quality control people.

In the steel mill, this following lesson was also learned quickly. An open-hearth melter with thirty plus years of experience was not always happy listening to his work critiqued by a young college graduate with minimal practice in the mill. Learning how to navigate this issue and others like it are not dissimilar to running a law firm and dealing with clients.

These lessons translated into my legal practice, because they taught me that whoever had contact with the client was in charge and, therefore, it was important to develop and maintain client relationships.

Stated simply, in small- and mid-sized firms, the smartest lawyer does not run the law firm, but the lawyer with the most client control does.

The other lesson learned was the importance of listening to people and being fair and open-minded when dealing with the daily problems. There is a delicate balance between being the boss and being able to get along with the employees.

Why did I leave the steel mill, where I was advancing nicely, being paid handsomely, and being promised all kinds of promotions? There are two answers to the question. The truth is the first, but I prefer the second.

The truth is that I spent four and a half years preparing for another career and I was not going to waste that opportunity.

The reason I give to those that ask is a bit far-fetched, but I like it. It goes like this:

Inland Steel was built on a huge landfill, extending into Lake Michigan. Number 3 Open Hearth extended the furthest into the lake, and had large openings at both ends so that the ingot cars could travel into the shop to a pouring platform, where a huge ladle containing the steel tapped from the open-hearth shop was teemed into multiple ingots. All of this took place with both ends of the open-hearth shop being open. In the winter months, the cold air came in from Lake Michigan and there were routinely below freezing temperatures. As I stood on the pouring platform in front of the steel teeming ladle, the heat radiation caused a redness of my face and sweat coming off my eyebrows. I would then look over my shoulder to the back of my open-hearth jacket where there were icicles hanging down caused from the blowing cold wind off the lake. I then, being a good engineer, calculated the ΔT, that is the difference in temperature between my face and my rear end and determined that the ΔT was far too great to continue with that particular occupation. Anyway, that is my story on why I left the steel mill and I stick to it.

Chapter VII

Law School Days

Why did I decide to go to law school in the first place? When I arrived at Inland Steel for my early indoctrination, I found that I was one of maybe a half dozen or so metallurgical engineers, along with many other chemical and industrial engineers who had been hired by Inland. I wanted to separate myself from this group, so I thought an advanced education would be the right way to go. In those days, many graduate employees who wanted to improve themselves went to the University of Chicago for their tremendous business school. I thought I would go in the other direction and further separate myself from the group, so I investigated various law schools. There were two or three night law schools in Chicago, and I determined that John Marshall Law School would be the best choice since they had the highest ranking in terms of law schools with students passing the Illinois bar.

I really did not enjoy law school. I had no time between my full-time job and school to properly study and/or enjoy the many opportunities going to law school provided. Fortunately, the analytical skills I learned during engineering school were a blessing and assisted in allowing me to figure out how to get through.

In my freshman evening class, there were one hundred thirty-four students starting law school. Of that number, seventeen (including myself) graduated. There were freshman students with varying backgrounds from policemen to teachers to rabbis and priests. Everyone had the same idea of putting another notch in their belt as they moved forward in whatever job they happened to hold. Many of the night freshman class had easy or no day jobs and had time to study and do the other things that I was unable to do.

My days went as follows. I went to the mill early in the morning and worked until four thirty or five o'clock in the afternoon. I then drove to Hammond, Indiana from East Chicago where the steel mill was located. I got on the South Shore train to downtown Chicago, and from there walked to John Marshall Law School, which was located on Plymouth Court in the heart of downtown Chicago. I attended class and afterwards got back on the South Shore train and arrived back in Hammond, Indiana and drove to my home in Munster, Indiana, getting there around eleven o'clock at night. I would wake up the next morning and repeat the same cycle. This went on for four and a half years until I finally graduated.

The law school was run by Dean Lee, who was a real tyrant. He taught a few classes, one of which was Illinois Constitutional Law. I, along with most of those who took his course, received failing marks on the first go-around and had to repeat the class. That was the reason for the additional half year past the anticipated four-year period for law school.

Dean Lee taught a few other classes and he was known for yelling at his students, throwing erasers at them, and making students stand up every time they responded to one of his questions. Many students were intimidated by this, but it did not bother me at all. I found it very useful to get up on my feet and argue with him, as I later did as a lawyer for most of my adult life.

I find it interesting that I do not remember a single professor from law school other than Dean Lee. This is contrary to the many high school teachers and college professors, who I still remember and to whom I owe a debt of gratitude. Law school was just another job that I had to complete with my nose to the grindstone. In reality, it served me well for the fifty-four years I spent practicing law.

Following graduation, I took and passed the Illinois bar exam and became a member of the State Bar of Illinois. I continued working in the steel mill for almost two years before I made the career change that I will discuss next.

Chapter VIII

Part-time Lawyer

After I received a job offer from Webb, Burden, Robinson, and Webb, Sue and I returned to Pittsburgh to find a place to live. I had checked the locations where all the existing lawyers worked and decided we would live in the part of town furthest from all them. We therefore bought a little house on Cornwall Drive in O'Hara Township for the grand total of $27,500.00. I went back to Chicago and shortly thereafter I went on a fishing trip to Canada with my buddies while my wife and my mother moved us from Munster, Indiana to our new address in Pittsburgh. We sent the truck to the new address, but Sue proceeded to send my mother home and then go to her home in Wellston, Ohio. I returned from my fishing trip and came to Pittsburgh without Sue. I had a two-week rental on the North Side of Pittsburgh and I walked to work across the Ninth Street Bridge. My first week with the firm was exciting because the second day, my car was stolen from the North Side, which I got back two days later, although all my wife's jewelry had been stolen out of the trunk. Fortunately, she did not have a whole lot of jewelry in those days so there was no great loss. When I got my car back from the police, after work I decided I would go look at the new house where I had put all of the money I owned to make sure it was ready for Sue and the furniture to arrive. Unfortunately, I could not find the house that I had bought and so I had to return and attempt to find it the next day which, fortunately, I did.

Webb, Burden, Robinson and Webb traced its origin to William Bakewell, who started practicing patent law in 1845 in Western Pennsylvania. My firm went through a number of name change iterations as partners died and new partners came on. For the last many years, it is simply known as The Webb Law Firm. It remains the oldest intellectual property law firm in the United States.

My first year or so was interesting as I learned an entirely new profession and had to adjust to all the differences between, for all practical purposes, being on my own and working within a large corporate environment. Although I had passed the Illinois bar a year or so before, there was no reciprocity and I had to take the Pennsylvania bar, along with all the other newbies. Fortunately, there was a bar review class taught by Levin Sarner and, after having taken that for the summer, I was able to pass the Pennsylvania bar on the first go.

I recognized from the outset that it was important to develop one's own clients and to do so one had to participate with the Allegheny County Bar Association ("ACBA") as well as many community activities where you could make your presence known. I joined the Arts and Law Section of the ACBA and found that quite interesting. The other members were general lawyers who had an interest in the arts and this was a good way to meet a lot of people with interests like mine and who could possibly send me their IP work.

I was invited to speak to the Copyright Club at the Federal Western Penitentiary just off downtown Pittsburgh. This seemed like a good opportunity to serve the public so I readily accepted the offer and proceeded one Saturday to the Penitentiary, where I went through all the entry protocol including being strip searched and the like. Following my inspection, the guard took me to the entrance to the open courtyard, where there were many inmates shooting baskets, lifting weights and, in general, glaring at me. The guard told me to walk across the courtyard into an alley and go up a flight of stairs and the Copyright Club was waiting for me on the second floor. I thought a better idea was that the guard should walk with me across the courtyard into the alley, which he readily agreed to do. I got into the meeting area and there were twenty plus inmates sitting there with all kinds of questions about copyrights, and they seemed truly interested in what I was saying. The President of the Copyright Club asked very good questions and, after forty-five minutes or so, I had completed my presentation and was prepared to leave. The inmate who was the President of the Copyright Club asked for my business card, and I made my first big mistake as a young lawyer. I gave him my business card. For the next two years, I received mail from almost every inmate in Western Penitentiary, telling me they were innocent and asking for my assistance to help get them out of there. Big mistake, but I learned my lesson.

In 1968, with the unfortunate death of Dr. Martin Luther King, Jr., we had riots in the Pittsburgh area. I volunteered to go into the toughest area of Pittsburgh, the Hill District, and agreed to work the midnight shift to make sure that all the people were being treated fairly and there was no unnecessary harming of the hordes of people who were coming into the police station for one reason or another. Most of the people were older Black people, afraid for their lives because the young people were rioting in the streets. Shortly after I arrived for the midnight shift, someone came into the police station and said that a young lady was lying on a pool table across the street in one of the bars and was giving away sexual favors to whoever wished to participate. The desk sergeant sent one of the policemen over to get her and, moments later, he came dragging her back into the police station. She had absolutely no clothing on and they opened one of the jail cells and threw her in and clanged the door shut. She immediately climbed on the bars, still completely naked, yelling every profanity she could at everyone who was there to listen. Finally, she went to sleep. When my shift was over in the morning, the desk sergeant said to me that the young lady had sobered up and that she lived in the neighborhood, and would I be so kind as to drop her off at her house. He had a twinkle in his eye. I respectfully declined and that was the end of my eight-hour stay in the Hill District. I spent the next midnight to eight o'clock shift in the police station in East Liberty. Again, there was constant activity but the police acted professionally and there really was not much for me to do other than to observe and to lend assistance where I could.

A. Domestic Clients

Most intellectual property (IP) law firm clients comprise small- to large-sized companies. There are very few individual inventors in the client base of most IP law firms. Some IP law firms do not take individual inventors because it usually is not cost effective to do so. I was just the opposite and liked the individual inventors. Realistically, they made up a very small part of my practice, but they were there nonetheless. An individual inventor got the standard lecture from me as follows.

> You do not have to spend any additional effort worrying about the legal end of protecting your invention. You have come to the right place and we can attend to that for you. The far greater issue for you to deal with is how are you going to market your invention? I simply do not want to take your money and get you a patent if all you are going to do is hang it on a wall and look at it. In other words, you need a business plan.

I would often send the client to a friend of mine at the University of Pittsburgh, Dr. Dennis Slevin, from the Graduate School of Business, who would assist the individual in developing a business plan.

No better example of this is that of Jess Peachey. Jess Peachey was an Amish man who lived in Bellville, Pennsylvania in the middle of Amish country in north central Pennsylvania. I obtained two patents for him, both of which he was able to turn into a financial gain.

The first invention was a grip for a hydraulic grease gun. Since Jess is Amish and does not drive, he had a neighbor drive him to my office, all the way from Bellville. When he and his neighbor showed up in my office, Jess described the invention to me, and I proceeded to take the necessary notes. I was happy to hear that he had a nice business plan in place to sell this product. He then left my office and I was intending to proceed with the preparation of a patent application on the invention disclosure he had given me. However, he returned to my office one hour later, explained that he and his neighbor had come to Pittsburgh in a red pickup truck that they had parked on the street, but they could not find it. We spent the rest of the afternoon walking the streets of Pittsburgh until we came across their truck. Finally, Jess and his neighbor could proceed back to Bellville. Jess set up a company called Jiffy Grip Co. LLC and continues to sell that product on the Internet and elsewhere.

Jess' second invention had involved a type of combine-like machine. The idea seemed unique and I was able to obtain another patent for him. His business plan involved licensing the patent to an appropriate company. He had already contacted New Holland in central Pennsylvania, a company that made farm equipment. Jess arranged a meeting and invited me to come with him to assist in negotiating and preparing an appropriate patent license agreement. I drove to a motel the night before and, the following morning, Jess's neighbor dropped him off and Jess was now in my hands. We went to New Holland and had a very good meeting and were able to successfully conclude a very reasonable license agreement.

As we left the meeting, Jess was very pleased and he said to me, "Russ," as he pointed to one of the nearby mountains, "Do you want to go up there and shoot a turkey, or would you rather go to my trout stream and catch some trout?" That was a difficult choice but, since I had recently had an operation on my knee, I chose the trout stream. We proceeded to the trout stream, I got out my fly rod with all my fancy flies and caught a trout or two over the next half hour. Thereafter, Jess came up to me and said, "What are you using, Russ?" and I showed him my fancy flies. He politely took my line, removed the fly, tied a hook on the line, and reached into his pocket and brought out a little jar of mealworms. Jess's principal business was that of a lumber company and mealworms are common place in the saw dust piles. Using mealworms, I then caught around twenty trout over the next couple of hours.

When I returned to Pittsburgh, with great glee I went to my local fly shop, International Angler in Aspinwall, Pennsylvania, and told those elitist fly fishermen that the way to catch trout was with mealworms. Thereafter, every time I went to International Angler, they would tease me and I would again explain to them that if you want to catch trout, use mealworms.

At the other end of the spectrum was Herman Myers. Herman owned an auto mechanic shop in Masontown, Pennsylvania. He had no formal education, but he had a tremendous inventive mind and was able to come up with fifteen to twenty new types of hand tools, all very good ideas and all very practical, over several years. The problem was that Herman was a bit of an egomaniac and he had no real plan to commercialize his products. Obviously, he needed money to get the fifteen to twenty patents, and so he would solicit money from his friends, who would join in his venture, again without a clear business plan for success. On a couple of occasions, I went to Masontown and met the school teachers and other people that he gathered to give them the legal status of the various patents and patent applications I had obtained for Herman.

Again, the problem with Herman was he had no real business plan and he always ran out of money to pay for my legal services. One time, he offered me a relatively new Mercedes Benz that he had in his auto shop and I foolishly rejected it. In hindsight, that would have been a good barter and would have covered some of his many expenses. Finally, I could give him no more credit and, when he called and told me that he needed me to write a contract, I told him, "Herman, you know Dee, our receptionist at the front desk. If you come to our door, you can knock but do not come in. I want you to put twenty-five-hundred dollars in cash underneath the door and I have instructed Dee to count the money and if it is twenty-five-hundred dollars, I will let you in and I will do the contract for you." That seemed rather out-of-the-box at the time, but it was the only way I could get paid for our services.

At some point, he finally contacted Stanley Tools and other hand tool manufacturers, but he was never able to consummate a deal. Again, beginning with a business plan is absolutely necessary for a small-time inventor if he is going to be successful in any form of business venture.

That brings me to Simon Bastacky, who was one of my absolute favorite clients. He was in the battery business and owned a small battery shop hanging off a cliff on Bigelow Boulevard in Pittsburgh. He was an immigrant from Poland who had been a Polish airplane pilot in World War II and was captured by the Germans and became a prisoner of war. He received preferential treatment from the German officers because he would jimmy their batteries on their vehicles so that they could not go out into the field where, toward the end of the war, most of them did not want to be.

Simon had a couple of nice little inventions relating to batteries. Because he was very cost conscious, he would call and invite me to lunch in the Oliver Building where my office was located. Simon thought that since he bought me lunch, we could do all our legal business over lunch and then he would only have to pay for lunch and nothing else. I went along with this because I liked him and I saw that his developments had potential.

Simon would appear in my office and his clothes would be full of holes from the battery acid from his shop.

I was having trouble getting one of his patents through the Patent Office and decided that we needed to go to Washington to interview the Examiner. Because there was some chemistry involved in the reactions of his battery and he was not high tech on the chemistry side, I arranged for us to visit a professor of chemistry at the University of Pittsburgh. We made that visit and the professor was kind enough to write out all the chemical reactions that were happening and gave us the technical reasons for the success he was obtaining in his batteries.

The day we were to go to Washington, DC, I went to the airport and got on the airplane and left an empty seat beside me for Simon. Just before the airplane was ready to take off, Simon came running onboard with a cup of coffee. He looked immaculate for the first time. There were no holes in his clothes and he was dressed in a nice pair of slacks and a sport jacket. As he approached me, he leaned over and said he had the chemistry information from the professor and wanted to give it to me. He put the coffee cup between his teeth and reached into his pocket to give me the written documentation from the professor. Unfortunately, the coffee slipped out of his mouth right into his crotch and now he not only had a burnt crotch but his clothes also looked like they normally did when he came to my office, this time with coffee stains and not battery acid holes.

When we got to Ronald Reagan Washington National Airport in Washington, DC, he proceeded to put his business card on the battery of every electric vehicle we saw in the airport. That was quite embarrassing because he usually had to lift the hood up high in the air to get to the battery. We got through that and went on to our interview.

I was familiar with the Examiner we were going to interview and he had the reputation for being a real hard ass. We walked into his office and he glared at the two of us like we were just wasting his time and we were not going to get anywhere with him. I tried to use all my legal talents to explain to him why the patent claims were patentable, and he was having nothing to do with that. I could see this was going to be an unsuccessful trip and I was a bit lost, so I pulled out the POW card. I casually mentioned that Simon had been a POW in World War II and gave him a little of Simon's history. Suddenly, the Examiner had a great smile on his face and proceeded to tell us that he had been in the service in World War II and was stationed someplace in the South doing secret government work. Even though it was now fifty years after the fact, he was not prepared to disclose anything to us because he said it was confidential. For some reason, he said something to Simon in either Polish or Russian, and Simon answered in the same language. The two of them had this wonderful discussion. They were both happy; they were both new friends, and everything looked like it was headed in the right direction. I looked at my watch and realized that our airplane would leave in about an hour and a half, and we had to get out of there, so I said to the Examiner that this had been a wonderful meeting, is there something that we can do to these claims to get this patent allowed? By then, he said to his new friend, "Oh, yeah, we can." and he gave me a few minor suggestions, all of which I had already made to him. I did that and the Examiner allowed the patent.

When we finally got the patent, Simon was so happy that he and his wife took Sue and me to the New China Inn for a tremendous dinner to celebrate the obtention of the patent.

Simon was able to commercialize the new product but unfortunately, he passed away and I doubt that he ever received the full value of the advances in the art he had made.

Another wonderful character and client was Alex Hrebeniuk from Sugar Run, Pennsylvania, which is in the central part of the state. Alex was from Russia and his wife was from Germany. He had been a plant breeder in Russia and, when he came to the United States, he continued to breed new varieties of poinsettias. He was referred to me by Dr. Richard Craig, one of the head plant horticultural professors from Penn State, and by Bob Oglevee, who owned Oglevee Floral, which I will discuss later. I would visit Alex at his little greenhouse in Sugar Run. It was essentially a four-hour drive for me, so it was not always convenient to get there, but I always made a point to go. He would show me the new varieties. We would go through the technical data sheets and then his wife would give me this scrumptious dinner of German food and beer. Every time, I was so tired I would have to stop halfway home and sleep because I could not drive four hours without falling asleep after being heavily sedated with this wonderful food and beverage.

Alex was using a popular plant food made by DuPont. It so happened that the last batch of plant food that DuPont had manufactured was outsourced to another company, who often did outsource work for them. Unfortunately, that company had previously run a pesticide through their manufacturing line and, when they ran the plant food, it got contaminated by the pesticide. DuPont ended up getting sued by a number of large farms and other horticultural businesses since they lost their entire crops. Alex, on the other hand, had lost several new poinsettia varieties through this infected plant food. I contacted Dr. Richard Craig to prepare an appropriate affidavit citing what had occurred and then went to DuPont with a claim that Alex had lost his breeding poinsettias due to contamination and that there was great financial potential going forward had he been able to proceed with the continued development of these new varieties that he had lost. DuPont reviewed the materials and agreed to compensate Alex one million dollars. I had reviewed Alex's tax records for the previous five years and he had barely made a living. When I gave him and his wife the check for a million dollars, you never saw a happier couple in all your life. I was told that he took the money and immediately bought a Mercedes Benz, which he drove into the little town of Sugar Run and ran into someone. Unfortunately, the day he bought his Mercedes, he also had his first car accident.

Subsequently, with the consent of Alex and Bob Oglevee, I arranged for the sale of Alex's poinsettia business to Oglevee Floral. It was a win-win for both parties.

Oglevee Floral and Bob Oglevee were my first introduction to plant patents in the 1970's. At that time, Oglevee Floral had fifty percent of the geranium business in the United States. They were growing their geraniums in Atlanta, Georgia and in Puerto Rico, but their main operation was in Connellsville, Pennsylvania. Bob Oglevee and his many business acquaintances bred new varieties of geraniums. Bob and his daughter, who had an advanced degree in horticulture and ran the laboratory, would collect all the required data and invite me out to review the information, look at the varieties, get the necessary pictures, and proceed with the plant patent applications on these new geranium varieties. I always enjoyed going there because each visit ended with us either going fishing on the local trout stream or going grouse hunting, which was one of Bob's favorite hobbies and something that I also thoroughly enjoyed.

Bob and his daughter had developed a unique system to ensure the cleanliness of the mother plants from which all other plants for further propagation and sale were taken. It involved a heating process and was known as Culture Virus Indexing (CVI®). All the greenhouses and companies that bought geraniums from Oglevee were required to sign a sub-propagator agreement, which I prepared, and which they agreed to comply with the growing and clean plant provisions. The clean plant provisions required that Oglevee products be grown in separate greenhouses from all other plants and that limited people could enter the greenhouse, rinse their feet in a special solution at the entry end of the greenhouse, and use only specially-cleaned implements, etc.

A licensee in Washington state reported his Oglevee geraniums had Xanthomonas pelargonium, a dreaded disease that could spread rapidly and wipe out a complete crop. Bob's son-in-law was the service representative for Oglevee, and he and I jumped on a plane and headed for Washington state. When we got there, we met with the owner and carefully inspected the greenhouse facility. It appeared to be in complete compliance with the license requirements. We noticed a large pile of dead plants at the far end of the property, and we knew the owner also sold Fisher geraniums, which were imported from Germany. We sat down with the owner in his living room and were greeted by a huge bushy Saint Bernard, who put his big, dirty, bushy head right on my lap. The source of the dreaded disease was obvious. The dog rolled in the pile of dead vegetation and had free access to all the greenhouses, where he was everyone's friend. The owner had gone to get us a cup of coffee and the son-in-law and I looked at each other, wondering which one of us would tell the owner to shoot the dog. The owner agreed to keep the dog out of the Oglevee greenhouse, although the damage had been done at a great negative cost to all involved.

Although Taylor-Wilson was not a huge client of mine, I have included them because this was my first experience in dealing with the Japanese. Taylor-Wilson was owned by Mr. McConnell and run by Mr. Bradley. They were very nice people who manufactured pipe testing equipment, so my background from the steel mill was very useful. Mr. McConnell would often invite me out to the plant when he had a new development. He would immediately take me to lunch at Shannopin Country Club, where he would ask the waiter for a cloth napkin, upon which he would use a pen to draw his latest invention. I would then take the napkin back to my office and was expected to turn a patent application out from the disclosure given to me on the cloth napkin. It worked since I understood the technology and was able to give him what he needed.

Taylor-Wilson then wanted to enter into a business relationship with a Japanese company that owned some United States patents. The Japanese company, represented by its President and another employee, came to Pittsburgh to meet with Mr. McConnell and Mr. Bradley in the downtown offices of Taylor-Wilson. We had arranged for a translator. I was there to assist with the negotiation with the Japanese company and prepare any necessary documentation.

Before any negotiation took place, the President of the Japanese company, through the translator, said he wanted to visit the plant. We then got into a car and drove out to McKees Rocks where the Taylor-Wilson manufacturing facility was located. The President of the Japanese company walked through the facility, handing out cigarettes to all the machine operators, not unlike what the United States soldiers did in World War II as they entered towns in Europe.

After touring the plant, we returned to the downtown offices and I started the negotiation with the President through the translator. The negotiations went on for at least an hour and a half with no give and no real negotiation on the part of the President of the Japanese company, as he remained totally firm on what he wanted. Finally, in exasperation, I took my wallet out and said, "You want everything from Taylor-Wilson. Do you want my wallet too?" and I put my wallet in front of him. "Here, take my wallet and whatever money is in it," I said. He had a little grin on his face and from there we proceeded to negotiate what I thought was a reasonable business arrangement. I knew I would have one chance to get a signature, so I said to Mr. Bradley, Mr. McConnell, and the Japanese President that I would go back to my office and prepare an appropriate Letter of Intent that could be signed by both parties. As I was leaving, I saw the President reach into his briefcase, pull out a bottle of high-priced scotch, and begin pouring drinks. I went back to my office and in about an hour I was able to put together the Letter of Intent. I returned to the Taylor-Wilson offices only to find everyone, including the secretaries and staff members, half inebriated as they were on their second bottle of scotch. I handed the Letter of Intent to the Japanese President to get his signature. Through the translator he informed me that he wanted me to go to the airport with him, so I went to the airport. In those days, you could go right to the concourse since you did not have to go through security. We got all the way to the gate where his plane was getting ready to take off and I could see that he was going to sit in first class and his associate was going to be in coach. He took out a pen, looked at me, and said in perfect English, "Mr. Orkin, I appreciate all the work you have done," and he proceeded to sign the Letter of Intent and give it to me as he climbed on the plane and departed for Japan.

That was my first experience dealing with the Japanese culture, and it proved very helpful as I spent the next thirty to forty years working with many Japanese companies.

My next story involves Sun Pacific, the number two citrus producer from the state of California. Berne Evans is the President of Sun Pacific, and was the person who hired me after I had been recommended by an associate of Sun Pacific from Philadelphia, for whom I had done some work. I proceeded to have a very good relationship with Sun Pacific and Berne. He was a very tough and successful businessman, always looking for opportunities for his business. This is where I came in, as I was asked to either assist in negotiating contracts or in doing due diligence to check out the history and legal worthiness of new citrus or grape products that Sun Pacific was about to introduce through a business relationship. My firm and I represented Sun Pacific in a number of litigation matters, all of which were extremely interesting and unusual since they involved either citrus or grape products as opposed to machinery and other types of products and services we think of as being patented.

One Monday, I received a call in Pittsburgh from Berne, instructing me to come to New York on the upcoming Saturday to negotiate a contract with the king of Morocco over new citrus varieties that had been developed there. Saturday morning, I got on a flight to LaGuardia and proceeded to the Plaza Hotel where Berne had a very large suite for the negotiation. It turned out that we were not meeting with the king of Morocco, but the head of the Ministry of Agriculture. Agriculture contributes fifteen percent of the Moroccan GDP and employs forty percent of the nation's work force so business relationships of this type are of extreme importance to the country.

We did manage to negotiate and complete an agreement and everyone went away happy.

I spent the better part of twenty winters in California, so I had a lot of direct contact with Sun Pacific and Berne Evans. He was an avid golfer and was a member of the Eldorado Country Club, which was founded in 1957 in Indian Wells. It was the home of President Eisenhower and many others. On my first trip to Eldorado Country Club, I was given a locker by the locker room attendant. As I was putting on my golf shoes, I noticed that a sign on the locker next to me said Bob Hope and a sign on the locker above me said Gerald Ford. I was in august company.

Berne could not have been nicer to me and often he would have Sue and me out to play golf with him and whoever he was with at the time.

Berne was very competitive and a decent golfer, and he liked to play for money. I was not accustomed to playing for money, but he was the client so here was my compromise. I said to him, "Berne, you have this wonderful ego and need to play for a lot of money. I myself play a $1 Nassau and occasionally I played a $5 Nassau, but I understand your need to play for a lot of money, so here is what I have to offer you. I will play for whatever you want. If you want to play for a hundred dollars a hole, I will play for a hundred dollars a hole; whatever you want is fine with me. Just understand one thing: the next bill you get from the Webb Firm, look under Miscellaneous Expenses and whatever amount I have lost to you will appear as a Miscellaneous Expense." He roared at that and it further cemented our relationship. He invited me to be his partner in a Member-Guest, which I thought was a wonderful thing to do since I was eighty years old at the time and my golfing skills were behind me.

Another unique client and individual was the Jennmar Corporation and Frank Calandra, its President. Jennmar Corporation is in the business of making mine roof bolts and other equipment for the mining industry. My first encounter with Jennmar was when Jennmar and Frank Calandra sued my client, H&S Machine and Frank Locotos, over a mine roof bolt on which Jennmar held a patent. At that time, Jennmar was the fifth or sixth largest mine roof bolt manufacturer in the world and my clients were just a small local operation with H&S manufacturing the product and with Frank Locotos being the salesman for the company. On behalf of my clients, I fought Jennmar tooth and nail for six years in the Western District of Pennsylvania before Judge Justin Johnson. We finally were able to settle the case before the trial date. On the day we settled the case, Frank Calandra called me and asked me to represent his company. I knew my clients were small and were about to go out of business, so I told Frank that if they continued to be in business, I would continue to represent them but I would check with H&S and get back to him. I called Ed Hipkins at H&S and he confirmed that he was going out of business because his son did not want to take over responsibility and he was getting old. He advised me to take Jennmar as the client as it was all right with him. On that basis, I contacted Frank and became their attorney for the next thirty or forty years.

Frank was a very tough guy and a very astute businessman. He went out of his way to hire the best people and he backed them to the hilt as long as they were accomplishing the objectives that were established by Frank. I felt he trusted me implicitly and, on occasion, he would call me to do personal favors such as going to the Civic Arena and entertaining his biggest client, Consolidated Coal Company, at a hockey game. During the time I represented Jennmar, they moved from where they were to having the largest mine roof bolt business in the world. I believe they had seven facilities in the United States and in a number of foreign countries, with two plants in Australia and one in Canada.

Frank was a firm believer that you had to sue your competitors from time to time to show them who was boss. As a result, Jennmar often got sued by companies that were out to retaliate. One such lawsuit involved the second largest mine roof bolt manufacturer who sued Jennmar in Australia over an Australian patent. This lawsuit dragged on indefinitely and Frank was getting very tired of having to deal with it.

He finally said to me, "Go jump on an airplane and go to Australia. I will give you a quarter of a million dollars to spend on the settlement of this lawsuit; see if you can settle it and make it go away." I then went to Australia and met with the Jennmar Australia company executives. At that time, they had an employee named Mick Wilkes from Liverpool, England, who had a long history of being in the coal business. As I talked with Mick, I felt more and more confident that there was a piece of prior art that he believed existed in the Liverpool, England area that would demonstrate that the patent we were being accused with was not valid. I listened closely and took all the details from Mick and returned to Pittsburgh without settling the lawsuit. I said to Frank, "I believe there is prior art that will invalidate that patent, so if you would authorize me to send one of my young associates to Liverpool, England with Mick, they will go through the records there to try to find this damning piece of prior art that we could rely upon." Frank liked the idea, so I went back to my office and I asked Nate Prepelka, one of our young attorneys, if he was prepared to go to England to search for this prior art. Nate was a soccer player and had just busted up his knee, so he was on crutches, but would not bypass that opportunity, so crutches and all he jumped on an airplane and met Mick. The two spent two or three days in the Liverpool area looking for this prior art, hitting all the pubs, drinking beer, and eating all the fish and chips they could. However, when they returned, they had the piece of prior art with all the necessary documentation authenticating it. I passed this on to the attorneys for the other side in Australia and they proceeded to drop the lawsuit with no damage adjustment.

I was able to settle a number of patent infringement lawsuits favorably for Jennmar and was able to cover our year-to-year legal fees to Jennmar many times over with the settlements from these lawsuits.

Another favorite client was Tippins, Inc. and George Tippins, its President. Tippins Machine Company was founded in 1923 by George's dad and known as Tippins and Springle Inc. Their original business was buying and selling used mining and steel mill equipment. Their offices were in Etna, a small town halfway between my office in downtown Pittsburgh and my home in O'Hara Township.

In the 1960's, George started developing new mill equipment, creating new modifications to the old Steckel mill rolling mill technology. The concept of a Steckel mill is to reduce the hot slab to an intermediate thickness in a roughing mill, and then pass the intermediate product back and forth through a four high reversing stand mill to the desired thickness. The product is kept hot by using coiling furnaces at either end of the four high reversing mill. The product is kept under tension during the rolling and coiling process.

The basic Steckel mill was developed by Ira Steckel at Cold Metal Process Co. in Youngstown, Ohio in the early 1950's. Our firm and Mr. William Webb represented Cold Metal Process and ended up bringing suit on the Steckel mill patent against many of the steel producers in the United States. These lawsuits, which were settled in the 1950's, resulted in excess of fifty-two million dollars in royalties paid to Cold Metal Process. That is why George Tippins came to Mr. William Webb with his interest in protecting improvements in the Steckel mill technology, and that is why Mr. William Webb turned George Tippins over to me since my background was in line with what George was in the process of developing.

Unlike most of my clients, George would not write out his inventions or fill out invention disclosure forms, but he would simply call me on the phone and say, "Hey Russ, stop out at the office on your way home; I have something I want to show you." The four high Steckel rolling mill consisted of two small work rolls to reduce the product and two larger backup rolls to drive the work rolls. Therefore, all I needed to take with me when I called on George was my yellow legal pad and fifteen cents, with the dime being the work rolls and the nickel being the backup rolls. With my dime and nickel, I could draw any invention George would disclose to me. Fortunately, the head of engineering and the successor to the Tippins business, John Thomas, was a wonderful engineer and would provide me with the necessary drawings and the other backup that George only passed over as he would explain his invention to me in his office after work hours.

Going to Tippins became my excuse to leave the office early. Our wonderful receptionist of many years, Dee Murgi, had the responsibility of knowing where all the attorneys were at any given time during business hours so, when I would leave early, I would say to Dee, "Going to Tippins!" whether I was or not. She would just look at me and smile.

I obtained twenty to thirty patents for Tippins, Inc. in which George Tippins and John Thomas were generally the primary inventors. We were able to enforce one of Tippins' Chinese patents against a Chinese company that was getting ready to use that technology. This is probably one of the few Chinese patents ever successfully enforced against a Chinese company by a US company.

One day, I received a call from George, and he said, "Hey Russ, the company has a little excess cash. Would you keep your eye out on any steel-related business, because I might need to invest this cash." I started looking for steel warehouses and small manufacturing companies related to the steel business to try to satisfy this need. The next thing I know, George bought Allegheny Ludlum Steel. I guess my sights were small compared to what George had in mind.

Unfortunately, George, who was one of the brightest people I have ever met in my life, developed Alzheimer's Disease and passed away from it. The company moved on to John Thomas, who ran it successfully for a short time before selling it to SMS Demag, a German machine manufacturing company.

My favorite client was Alec Keith. Alec had been a Korean War fighter pilot. In 1952, he came down with polio. 1952 was the same year that Jonas Salk discovered the vaccine for polio at the University of Pittsburgh, but it was too late to save Alec. Alec lost the use of both of his legs and one of his arms and was wheelchair bound from 1952 to the present.

Alec had worked for one of the big New Jersey pharmaceutical companies and had been instrumental in developing the transdermal patch technology, which enabled a medicament to pass directly into the bloodstream through the skin from the patch, thereby bypassing the stomach, which carries all the many ramifications with it. He eventually moved to State College, Pennsylvania, where he formed Zetachron, Inc., a company dedicated to research and development of products like the transdermal delivery products upon which he had previously worked. I was introduced to Alec through the Seton Company, who had used him as an expert witness in some early litigation for them. Alec became a very good client and we obtained several patents for him when he owned and operated Zetachron. Zetachron was then acquired by Watson Pharmaceuticals from Corona, California. At the time, Watson Pharmaceuticals was the largest generic pharmaceutical company in the United States. Alec became president of Watson Pharmaceuticals and I proceeded to represent Watson Pharmaceuticals with many of its intellectual property issues.

Alec retired from Watson Pharmaceuticals and moved to Hilo, Hawaii to a beautiful home overlooking the ocean, where he was able to watch the whales go by. He had signed a five-year noncompete agreement with Watson when he left, so I did not hear from him for five years. At the end of his noncompete, he called me and said, "Hey Russ, I have been developing new products and technology over the last five years at my lab here in Hilo, and I would like you to come out and we can go over these developments that I have made." I said, "Alec, I would be happy to send my team of biotech attorneys to work with you on getting the disclosures for the various developments you have made, but you really do not need me to come shake your hand and have dinner with you." With that he said to me, "I just got my royalty check from Watson for this year in the amount of x million dollars." When I heard the number, I said, "I'll be out in a couple of weeks."

I then took Sue, Judy, and two biotech attorneys from my office and off we headed to the Big Island of Hawaii. Sue, Judy, and I went a day or two early and went to the Kona Coast, on the opposite side of the Big Island from Hilo. The Kona Coast is the home of Kona coffee, which is famous worldwide. We had a great time exploring the Kona Coast and all it had to offer to tourists. The day I was to travel to Hilo for the meeting, I woke up early and found that I could not hear, which meant I had a wax buildup in my ears, a problem I dealt with most of my life. As I stumbled out of bed not being able to hear, I accidentally stepped on my glasses and broke them. I am now several hours away from one of the most important meetings of my life and I cannot hear or see. Judy happened to have one of her old nursing friends living in Hawaii. She was able to contact her and get me set up in a clinic to deal with my ear problem. Judy and Sue dropped me off at the clinic to have my ears cleaned of wax, and they took off looking for glasses for me. After an hour or so, they returned and asked the receptionist my location. The receptionist got on a speaker and said, "Where is the ear?" This cracked Judy and Sue up, but they were able to locate me with clean ears and a new pair of glasses for my big meeting with Alec in Hilo.

I met the two lawyers from my office in Hilo and we went to Alec's home, which was beautifully positioned, overlooking the ocean. In the back of his house was a huge laboratory, which he had access to through walkways that were easily navigated with his wheelchair. We went to the lab and Alec was in a good frame of mind, so we laughed and joked about good times we had in the past. He brought out a blow gun and shot darts across the lab into some target he had set up in the ceiling, much to the pleasure of myself and my lawyers. He had distilled some alcohol and convinced the two female attorneys to have a drink or two with him. I passed on the matter, knowing that this was not headed in a good direction. Finally, when we got down to business, it turned out that Alec had kept a lab notebook for five years and it was filled with inventions. The unusual part of it was, to amuse himself, he had written the book starting from the back and working to the front, and he had written it in Greek. All of this was above my head, but fortunately the two attorneys were able to sit with him for hours and go through the disclosures, which they were able to translate into English. Once this was accomplished, we were able to obtain the necessary patent protection for him. He did not do this because he wanted to make money from the venture; he did it because he had made some developments in a number of areas and he was prepared to dedicate this technology for the use of whoever could benefit from it. When I last tried to contact Alec, I called him but did not receive an answer. An Internet search revealed that he was ninety-one years old and still going strong. I should note that one of his favorite hobbies was playing chess, and on many nights, he would play online with the world champion from Russia all night long; he became Alec's dearest buddy. Alec told me that he never lost to the Russian world champ, because they would play and play into the wee hours of the night and then the Russian champ would say, "Alec, I am tired. I am going to bed." At that point, Alec knew he was one move away from checkmate, but the Russian champ would never make the next move that would cause Alec to have been defeated. I think that is a wonderful story on which to end my business relationship with Alec Keith.

The R.I. Lampus Company was a family-owned business by Don Lampus, the founder's son. Don is a personal friend of mine, with whom I took several fishing trips. The company started in the concrete block business and, over time, expanded into paving stones and metallurgical products for the foundry industry.

In the early- to mid-80's, a dispute arose in the paving stone industry when a German citizen named Fritz van Langsdorf claimed to own the patent on the paving product manufactured by many companies in the United States. Some manufacturers chose to license and others, including the R.I. Lampus company, chose to ignore the patent.

A lawsuit was brought in Tampa, Florida by Fritz van Langsdorf against three US companies including my client. I was asked to represent those defendants, the other two being a company in West Palm, Florida and one in Cincinnati, Ohio. The trial took place in the United States District Court for the Middle District of Florida in Tampa.

Just prior to the trial, I had unintentionally lost seventeen pounds and was having sweating and tiredness issues. I had gone to a doctor, who ordered blood tests. Pam was graduating from high school and Judy and Mort arrived from Cleveland for the graduation. Mort took one look at me and sat me down for a whole series of questions. Judy, who was in nursing, came into the room and said to Mort in her quiet way that he could quit asking questions because she could tell from my eyes that I had hyperthyroidism. The blood test confirmed the correctness of her thirty second evaluation. I then went on a heavy medication to control it.

The trial proceeded but not smoothly because Fritz van Langsdorf, who spoke perfect English, insisted on testifying through a translator. This put added pressure on me because I had to slowly ask my cross-examination questions and my follow-up questions were often diluted and not as effective as they should have been under normal circumstances. During the morning of the third or fourth trial day, I started to break out in a cold sweat and felt terrible. At lunchtime, I went back to my hotel room and stood under a cold shower for thirty minutes or so. At the afternoon session, I had no choice but to tell the judge that I was on a medication that was not working and my associate, Rick Byrne, would take over for me.

The wily old attorney, Albert Johnson, for the plaintiff took full advantage and started asking leading questions one after another. Rick was a young lawyer and inexperienced in such matters. I could take it no longer and I jumped to my feet and said, "I object to the question as leading and, by the way, I am feeling better and will continue as the lead attorney." The judge got a big kick out of that, and I am sure Rick was relieved.

We won the case before the District Court, but lost on appeal in the Court of Customs and Patent Appeals (CCPA). My clients ended up taking a license after all, although I remain convinced that the CCPA was wrong.

Sometime in the early 1970's, Wayne Alderson was referred to me by Emil Hermann, a general practitioner in Pittsburgh. Wayne needed assistance in establishing a business plan to protect and promote his intellectual property. The intellectual property consisted of trademarks and documentation he had created in connection with his new labor management consulting firm.

Wayne had an amazing history. He grew up in Western Pennsylvania, the son of a coal miner, living in a company house. At age eighteen, he enlisted in the Army and was soon stationed in the Alsace-Lorraine region of France. His company had lost both of their advance scouts and needed a "point man." Wayne, as a lowly private, volunteered and, in March of 1945, became the first American to enter Germany and to attack the Siegfried Line, which was the first line of defense for the Third Reich. He was wounded in a trench by the shrapnel from a hand grenade and for the rest of his life had a dent in his forehead to show for his efforts.

In the 1950's, he attended night school at Robert Morris University (at that time known as The Robert Morris School), where he graduated with a degree in accounting and business administration. He started as the Controller of a steel foundry in Pittron, Pennsylvania, owned by Textron Inc. He eventually worked his way to Vice President in charge of operations. Following a labor strike, Wayne was able to reunite labor and management by meeting with the workers every day at lunchtime and, using the Bible as a guide, he focused on love, dignity, and respect for both labor and management.

In November of 1973, the Pittron foundry experienced a horrific fire and explosion. A ladle of molten steel got locked in the open position and steel started pouring over the entire floor area as the ladle moved out of control along the length of the trolley line. Somehow, the men on the floor and the crane operator were able to escape. Everything else was burned beyond belief except a Bible in a metal locker where the lunchtime meetings had taken place. Eventually the foundry was sold and Wayne lost his job. That was when he started his labor management consulting firm.

A number of businessmen from the Pittsburgh area wanted that story told, so they commissioned a movie called Miracle of Pittron. The movie, along with a trademark for Value of the Person® and training manuals, became the cornerstone of his business.

I took a large tin canister containing the movie to the Library of Congress in Washington, DC and registered the copyright in his and his wife Nancy's names. This proved most useful as, years later, certain third parties tried to claim ownership, but the copyright carried the day for Wayne.

I created a trademark license agreement that Wayne used with the various companies that retained him and it became a necessary source of income, along with his consulting fees, to keep the business going.

During and following his time in the service, he received a Purple Heart, Bronze Star, Silver Star, and other medals for his heroic service. With the assistance of the few living soldiers in Wayne's platoon, I sent a letter on Wayne's behalf to President Clinton, requesting that Wayne be given the Medal of Honor. President Clinton responded with glowing accolades to Wayne but said that the Medal of Honor was to go to an African American that year.

Wayne passed away in 2013 and his daughter, Nancy Jean McDonald, continues to run the business. It was a true pleasure to work with Wayne and his family for many years.

Every attorney that has ever tried a lawsuit has a favorite one that always comes to mind. My favorite lawsuit involved the Seton Company out of Newark, New Jersey. The lawsuit took place back in the 1980's, and Seton had become my client through Bob "Demo" DeMajistre, who had left our firm and gone to work for the Seton Company and ultimately became their president. In the 1980's when the lawsuit took place, Paul Fertel was the president and Philip Kaltenbacher, the son of the founder, was the principal owner of the company. Philip had been involved in New Jersey politics and, at the time of the lawsuit, was also chairman of the Port Authority of New York and New Jersey. That office was in the Twin Towers that were taken down on 9-11; fortunately, Philip was not there.

The Seton Company was in the leather tanning business. They had a number of tanneries around the country and they tanned cowhide into beautiful leather that was used in the auto industry for leather car seats. As they were growing in the 1980's, they also entered into a few healthcare-related businesses. One business was a joint venture company called Selomas. Selomas was formed as a joint venture between the Seton Company and Lohmannn GmbH, a German pharmaceutical and adhesive manufacturing company. The joint venture agreement, which was not prepared by our office, provided for Seton to sell and promote the products of Lohmannn GmbH through Selomas in the United States. While on a trip to Lohmann GmbH, Paul Fortell saw a new product, a small transdermal delivery patch, that was being developed by Lohmann GmbH. He took the small patch that he had been shown and attached it on the underside of his tie with a tie clip, and returned to the United States. Seton, through Selomas, attempted to get this technology introduced into the United States, but Lohmann GmbH would not have any of it. There was an arbitration provision in the joint venture agreement, so Seton initiated arbitration in 1987. The arbitration was to take place in New York City and, for the next two years, I spent the better part of my time in New York City trying this international arbitration.

There were three arbitrators that I will refer to as "French Arbitrator 1," "French Arbitrator 2," and "the American Arbitrator." French Arbitrator 1 was an attorney in "Wild Bill" Donovan's law firm that Donovan established in 1929 after leaving government as the founder of the CIA. That law firm was known as Donovan, Leisure, Newton & Irvine. Arbitration was held in their offices.

The arbitration was set up to be bifurcated, with the first part of the arbitration going to liability and then, if liability was found, the second phase of the trial, the damages, would be conducted. Lohmann GmbH hired a lawyer from New York City who was also a state senator in New York at the time. Apparently, they felt that it would be beneficial to have a state senator representing their company. The liability phase dragged on and off for the better part of a year and finally the decision came down finding liability on the part of Lohmann GmbH. We then set up the damages phase of the trial. At that time, transdermal delivery patches were just being developed with the patch for the heart and scopolamine for use behind the ear for motion sickness. There was tremendous potential, and our claim for damages was based not on the few patches that had already been developed but on the many patches that were projected to be developed in the future since that was exactly the purpose for which Selomas was created in the first place.

Lohmannn GmbH fired their state senator attorney and hired Stuart Meiklejohn from Sullivan & Cromwell, one of the most prestigious law firms in the country. Stuart had a great reputation as an antitrust lawyer and he turned out to be one of the brightest, if not the brightest, attorney I have ever met and have ever worked with albeit on opposite sides of a case. Stuart had no technical background, and I was absolutely amazed at how quickly he learned all the technologies involved and was able to successfully present his witnesses and successfully cross-examine our witnesses. The damages phase of the arbitration took place over the year 1988 and there were many weeks that I would travel to New York City with my partner Bill Logsdon on Monday morning and return on Friday night, only to repeat the trip the following week. Every Monday morning, we would meet before the arbitration started and discuss the schedule for the week. Stuart and his team of lawyers were always well-prepared and ready to go. Interestingly, the lowest ranking associate on the Sullivan & Cromwell team handling the litigation was being billed at a higher rate than me, and I was lead counsel for the Seton Company. When the Monday morning meeting would start, the arbitrators would ask what our schedules looked like for the week. Stuart Meiklejohn would pull out a leather-bound journal and thumb through it looking at his appointments and advising the arbitrators of his availability. I would reach in my wallet and pull out my son's basketball schedule to see if the Friday night game was one that I needed to attend so I could advise if I had to be home by late afternoon on Friday. The arbitrators were very understanding and things proceeded smoothly.

In one particular session when I was cross-examining one of Lohmann's key technical witnesses, I noticed that every time I had the witness in a corner, he seemed to know about it and would find a way to get out without answering my question. At the break, Demo told me that the general counsel for Lohmann was sitting in the back of the room next to the light switch and he would flick on the lights every time he saw that I was going to make points with the technical witness from

Lohmann. After our break, I approached the arbitrators and presented this information. Stuart Meiklejohn was likewise horrified that this had occurred and the arbitrators banned the general counsel for Lohmann from ever attending the arbitration proceeding again.

French Arbitrator 1 had family still in Europe and apparently wanted a free ride home, so the arbitrators announced that the arbitration should move to Germany because the arbitrators would like to go through the pharmaceutical facility of Lohmann GmbH to see where the product was being manufactured. We then all jumped on airplanes and traveled off to Germany to continue the arbitration. On our side was me, my partner Bill Logsdon, and Demo who was by then vice president of the Seton Company. We were staying in a small hotel several miles from where the Lohmann plant was located. Lohmann had extended us the courtesy of sending a driver to pick us up. The driver had a black patch over one eye and proceeded to drive on the Autobahn at speeds approaching 100 mph. The three of us firmly believe that this driver had been sent out to kill us before we could attend the rest of the arbitration. Fortunately, we arrived safely to the arbitration and went through the pharmaceutical facility, ending up in a large laboratory where the head of research for Lohmann was to make a presentation concerning the technology. He made the presentation in broken English, but it was nothing more than a brief that had obviously been prepared by Stuart Meiklejohn and his staff. This was starting to irritate the hell out of me and I had to find a way to give this a reality check. At the end of the presentation by Herr Wolf, Stuart Meiklejohn asked the arbitrators if they had any questions. The arbitrators had a few questions. French Arbitrator 1 turned to me and said, "Russ, do you have any questions for Herr Wolf?" Behind me in the laboratory was a huge picture typical of laboratories, this one having six monkeys in lab coats and they were working with test tubes and Bunsen burners. It was a very comical picture, not unlike others found in research laboratories. When it came time for my question, I pointed at this picture of these monkeys in lab coats and I said, "Herr Wolf, what did these gentlemen look like before you started working on them?" That absolutely cracked up the three arbitrators, Stuart Meiklejohn was fumbling, not knowing what to say, and my partner Bill Logsdon had his hands over his head, embarrassed by what he had just heard. However, I am completely convinced that the arbitrators understood the reason for me doing that and only gave small weight to the presentation of Herr Wolf.

An interesting witness for Seton was Brendon Byrne, the governor of New Jersey from 1974-1982. I spent a good deal of time prepping witnesses during the down time surrounding the arbitration hearing. Brendan was a practicing lawyer after his governorship who had been retained by the Seton Company to testify to certain financial transactions that he had handled for Selomas. The only time he had for prepping was in the back seat of a limousine on the way to the arbitration in mid-town Manhattan from his office in Newark. Much to my chagrin, he assured me he needed no prepping prior to testifying. He did a wonderful job on direct examination. At one point in his cross-examination, Stuart got him to agree to a number of facts and then hit him with a question along the lines of, "Weren't you surprised by the amount of money at stake?" Brendon looked at Stuart and said, "After eight years of being governor of New Jersey, nothing surprises me."

Stuart then took another tact with him on a Securities and Exchange Commission (SEC) issue. He again got Brendon to agree to a number of facts and then hit him with another question along the lines of, "Given the requirements of SEC Sections A, B, C, D, etc., how can you possibly justify your recommended course of action?" Brendon looked Stuart straight in the eye and testified, "If you want the answer to that question, you can come to my office, pay my retainer, and I will then give you my legal advice regarding that question." Stuart finally gave up and we moved on to the next witness.

At the completion of the arbitration, both sides had to file briefs. During that time, Lohmann GmbH had been offered an opportunity to build a plant in the United States to manufacture a transdermal patch for nicotine for smoking cessation. They therefore approached Seton and wanted to talk settlement before the award was granted.

This put all the bargaining power with us and, while Stuart Meikle-john was a brilliant lawyer, I was halfway decent myself, and was particularly good at fighting in the trenches in which we were now involved. The settlement was made in an amount of X million dollars and the Seton Company was more than well satisfied with the outcome.

Every time I am with a bunch of lawyers and we start telling these "Out of School" stories about things that have happened to us, I am quick to bring up the Seton arbitration and all the crazy things that occurred.

B. Foreign Clients

A number of our clients, particularly the larger ones, wanted to protect their inventions in countries other than the United States. The practice in those days was to take the US patent application that had been pre-pared by us and forwarded to a New York law firm, Ladas and Perry who, in turn, would send it to their foreign associates around the world and proceed to obtain foreign patents for our clients.

This practice did not make sense to me because we were, in effect, bringing in a middle man who was charging fees for their services and therefore the client was not only paying us and the foreign associate, but also paying the middle man in New York. I went to Mr. William Webb, the managing partner of the law firm and my mentor for the years I had been with the firm, and offered my services to go to Asia and Europe and develop our own foreign associates, thereby cutting out the middle man and therefore putting more money in our pockets and overall saving money for the client. He agreed wholeheartedly with the concept and so I became the official "shoe salesman" for The Webb Law Firm.

1. Asian Clients

I only had one contact in Japan and that was Mr. Matsui. Mr. Matsui came to our office on one of his trips to Pittsburgh, where he was representing US Steel in Japan. I therefore contacted Mr. Matsui and he readily agreed to my visit to his office in Tokyo. I asked around the office if anyone else had any contacts in Japan, and my partner, Bob DeMajistre, told me that he was negotiating a contract with the Japanese over baseballs and he gave me the name of the Japanese lawyer representing the other party. That law firm was the O. Kitamura Patent Office, and I noticed that they were in Osaka. Bob told me he thought Osaka was just outside of Tokyo and so I arranged to visit Mr. Osamu Kitamura in Osaka. It turned out that Osaka is quite a distance from Tokyo, and it necessitated me taking the bullet train to get there.

Over the next twenty or more years, I made numerous trips to Japan, South Korea, Taiwan, and once to Hong Kong. I always tried to take someone with me because these trips lasted two weeks and it was much easier to have someone with me than spend all that time alone in foreign countries. Sue went with me on my first trip and on many trips thereafter and, in addition, I was able to take our children, Brian or Pam. Jill only went to Europe with me and not Asia. In later years, I took lawyers from my office who had been doing most of the work and would inherit these clients.

My first trip to Mr. Kitamura's patent office in Osaka was quite an experience. Sue was with me and, after I found his office, I noted a hotel across the street. I told Sue to meet me in the hotel at noon and I went into Mr. Kitamura's office for my meeting. The first thing that occurred was that I was taken into a very small conference room with a very low table and the young lady who accompanied me into the room asked me to sit in one of the very low chairs. She then brought a cup of tea and set it in front of me. After several minutes, the door opened and she brought in an American flag, which she put in front of me, and a Japanese flag, which she put across from me where Mr. Kitamura was going to sit. She then left. After several more minutes, the door opened and in walks this elderly Japanese man, Mr. Kitamura, with about four translators with him since he spoke no English whatsoever. He bowed at me and I bowed at him and he sat down, barking orders to the translators. The first thing the translator said to me was that Mr. Kitamura wanted me to know that he had designed Japanese submarines in World War II. I have always been known for my sense of humor, and I could barely suppress the smile that wanted to come to my face because I knew that every Japanese submarine had ended up at the bottom of the ocean, but I managed to overcome any smile and nodded bravely to him. We then proceeded to have a very interesting business conversation, where we agreed to exchange work between us, with him sending work from Japan to our firm and me sending work from our firm to him in Osaka. As our meeting was coming to an end, through the translator he wanted to know if I was traveling by myself. I told him that I was traveling with my wife and she was waiting for me across the street. He immediately started barking out orders and the translators all started running in different directions, opening closets, collecting gifts, and all of us then got up and headed out of his building across the street into the hotel. I had several misgivings about what could occur because Sue normally is not on time for anything and I had no idea if she would be there or not. Fortunately, she was there sitting in the bar, drinking a beer, as Mr. Kitamura and his enclave approached. After bowing and exchanging gifts, one of the translators said that Mr. Kitamura had asked him to take Sue and me to the old Imperial capital of Kyoto, and he wanted us to visit many temples and shrines that he thought we would find interesting. We then got on the bullet train with the translator and headed off to Kyoto. I could see that the translator was very nervous, being given this responsibility. When we got to Kyoto, we started visiting temples and shrines and gardens and, after four or five, both Sue and I were exhausted, so I asked him if we could take a break here and go have a beer or something. He immediately got a smile on his face. He said he was from Kyoto and he was going to take us to lunch at his mother's restaurant. It was a Monday and we walked into this beautiful Japanese restaurant and not a soul was there. We finally figured out that the restaurant was closed on Monday and he had called his mother, who brought the whole staff in to cook us lunch. The gracious way we were treated that day persisted on every visit we took to Japan and the other Asian countries.

After we developed this wonderful relationship with Mr. Kitamura, he started sending great volumes of work to us with the principal client being Kubota Tractor Company. On many subsequent trips to Mr. Kitamura's office, we would often go and visit Kubota and do presentations to their legal department on US law and other requirements, in which they were very interested.

On one of my subsequent trips, I took one of my partners, Paul Reznick, with me since he was doing a great deal of the work for Kubota and other clients of Mr. Kitamura. I wanted Paul to have the full experience, so I arranged to stay in a Ryokan (a Japanese hotel) in Kyoto. Paul was a very bright and excellent lawyer, and a wonderful character as well. He was often slovenly dressed and, more often than not, there were coffee stains on his shirt. When we got to the Ryokan in Kyoto, it was clear that we were the only Caucasian people there and the hostess who greeted us spoke very little English. She took us up to our room and we told her we wanted to go to the Japanese baths in the hotel. She understood that and gave us robes and told us to undress and put on the robes, and we could then go to the Japanese baths, which were on the lowest floor in the hotel. As Paul and I were leaving our room, which consisted of two mats laying on the floor and no true mattresses, I noticed that his robe was partially opened and his privates were hanging out. Normally I would have said something but, since we were just headed down to the baths anyway, I figured it did not matter and I did not want to embarrass him. We got on the elevator and he pushed the button to go to the basement. The door opened and he got out and I heard this whole series of gasps of female voices. I looked out and we were in the gift shop and not the baths and all these women were standing there looking at Paul with his privates hanging out. I immediately grabbed him by the back of the neck and pulled him back into the elevator and we proceeded to our baths and they went on quite nicely. As we were going out to dinner, I stopped at the reception desk and arranged to have two masseuses in our room when we returned from eating, this being a standard custom in Japan. We got back from eating and again disrobed and donned our robes. There was a knock on the door and only one masseuse was there and she pointed to me and told me to lay on the mat. She then proceeded to jump up and down on my back, which caused me to start laughing and, the next thing I knew, there was another knock on the door and the second masseuse entered. She had Paul lay down right beside me and she jumped on his back. Paul and I laughed so hard we had tears in our eyes as these two Japanese girls were beating the absolute devil out of us. It was quite an experience as you can imagine.

On another trip to Japan, I took another of my partners, Rick Byrne, who succeeded me as President of our firm. Rick was very interested in the culture and so, since the bullet train went past Mount Fuji, I arranged for us to stay there to explore Mount Fuji and the surrounding area. The area was called the Hakone Area, and it was at the base of Mount Fuji. Rick and I stayed at a nice quaint hotel the first night, and had a wonderful meal. The next day we explored Hakone by following the directions given to us at our hotel. These directions included taking a train trip to a bus, and then taking the bus to a lake, and then taking a boat across the lake, the boat being some sort of a Pirate-looking ship.

We then got on a cable car and went up the side of Mount Fuji. We got lost on several occasions and, at one point in time, an English person on the bus told us we were going the wrong direction and we finally were able to get off the bus and get the yellow-colored bus that we had been told to look for, and head back to where we were going. By then, it had started to rain and so we were standing on a corner in the middle of nowhere with one umbrella. Since I was about six inches taller than Rick, we both ended up getting soaking wet.

On one of our trips to Tokyo, Mr. Matsui had inquired if anyone would be traveling with me. I informed him that my wife and daughter would be with me. He wrote back and said that he would have his wife and son take my family to the gardens while he and I conducted our business. We were greeted in the hotel where we were staying by Mr. Matsui and his wife, who was wrapped in a red kimono-type outfit and looked very charming. She and her son proceeded to take Sue and Pam to the gardens. The only problem was that my family did not speak Japanese and his family did not speak English, so they spent the better part of the day together not being able to communicate. The son was studying English and he would write some English but he could not speak it. At dinner that night, we sat again at a long low table with Sue, Pam, and me on one side and Mr. Matsui, his wife, and his son on the other side. The first course served to us was a little plate with some brown gooey stuff, which we proceeded to eat. That was taken away and they brought the second course, which was a little bowl of soup. My inquisitive wife, being very friendly and sociable, asked Mrs. Matsui what we had just eaten. Of course, Mrs. Matsui did not understand a word she said, so Sue turned to the son and asked him and he tried to scribble something down but he was not getting anywhere. At that point, Sue picked up her bowl of soup and started to drink it at the same time she asked Mr. Matsui what we had just eaten. He responded that, biologically speaking, it was testicles and ovaries. With that, Sue tilted the cup of soup and it went down the front of her dress. Neither she nor Pam could eat any more. We managed to struggle through the rest of that meal, but it was quite an experience.

On our very first visit to Japan when I was traveling with Sue, I arranged to see one of our clients, Japanese Electronic Optical, Limited (JEOL). They were located outside of Tokyo in what would be considered a suburban area. The head of intellectual property for JEOL had sent a young man to the Okura Hotel, where we were staying, which was located next to the US Embassy. The young man showed up and I departed with him heading for Tokyo Station, leaving Sue behind. We got to Tokyo Station and got on the train. I looked at my watch as we got on the train and it was 3:00 pm. At 4:00 pm we got off the train. We then went to the JEOL facility, which was a huge manufacturing operation of high tech, sophisticated electronic equipment for doing chemical testing and things of that type. Interestingly, all the workers were dressed identical to management and it was not possible to distinguish management from the work force. The only difference was that if management had an outside visitor such as myself, they were given the company car and were able to entertain. Following our meeting, the company car and the driver took me and the head of intellectual property for JEOL and one of his associates up into the mountains to a beautiful restaurant. We were under a thatched roof and were waited upon by a couple of young Japanese girls who were very well educated and engaged in conversation and provided us with food and drink. As I already knew, the Japanese are not very good at holding their alcohol and, after two or three drinks, the two Japanese associates with me were well on their way. We had an enjoyable dinner but, by the end of dinner, both of my companions had passed out. I put one under each arm and carried them to the car and told the driver to take me to the train station where they had picked me up. He took me there and dropped me off. It was now about 11:00 pm. In the early days, nothing was in English and so I had absolutely no idea which direction I should go to get back to the Tokyo Station. I finally figured out which direction to go and I got on the train. I knew it was about a one-hour trip and that the Japanese rail system was always punctual, so at midnight I got off the train and lo and behold, I was back at Tokyo Station where I started. By the time I got to the hotel room, Sue was worried because it was now one o'clock in the morning and she could not figure out where I had been and, of course, I did not know where I had been either, but it proved to be quite an interesting experience.

Our favorite law firm to visit was Dr. Suzuki's law firm in Tokyo. Dr. Suzuki had gone to UCLA and spoke perfect English. He had a twinkle in his eye and was always looking for a good time. On one of my trips that included my daughter, he fell madly in love with her and attempted to woo her as he continued to drink far too much sake. We got a big kick out of that, but he was a perfect gentleman.

On a subsequent trip to Dr. Suzuki's office, I had Brian with me. Brian is about 6'1" and 220 pounds and he towered over the Japanese. Dr. Suzuki, who could not get over Brian, had arranged for us to eat at a Shabu Shabu restaurant. This is a restaurant where you sit in front of a pot of boiling water and put thin pieces of meat into the boiling water for just a second or two. It is absolutely delicious. You do the same thing with a plate of vegetables that they bring to you. Because Brian was there, Dr. Suzuki brought two of the young girls from his office, who sat on either side of Brian and proceeded to cook his food for him and feed him. He just sat there with a big grin on his face. Across the table was Dr. Suzuki who, at one point said to me, "Mr. Orkin, I have learned a new drink that I enjoy." I asked him what it was and he replied, "I like vodka." I immediately knew that we were in trouble. He proceeded to have a couple of martinis and the next thing I knew, he fell forward and his face ended up in a bowl of rice that had been placed in front of him. He had whiskers on his face from the end of the day and when he jumped up, there had to be five hundred kernels of rice attached to the whiskers on his face. It probably was the funniest thing I had ever seen in my life and Brian and I could not stop laughing. By the end of the evening, we had eaten four platters of thinly cut and expensive Kobe beef, with Brian causing most of the damage. I can only imagine what that bill looked like.

On the many trips I took to Japan, I always made sure that Dr. Suzuki's office was the last stop because the next day was best served flying on an airplane and not visiting other clients.

On one of the trips when I was traveling to South Korea on my own, I visited Mr. Im and his law firm. It was a very small law firm and Mr. Im spoke virtually no English. He therefore had a young associate with him who translated throughout our meeting. When we went to dinner, he brought the young associate with him and he sat next to him and across from me. They initially brought each of us a plate with two snails on it. I happen to like escargot, so I figured I could handle eating these snails except, when I went to get the snail out of the shell, the snail crawled back into the shell. I looked at Mr. Im and he had taken his two snails and put them on the plate of his young associate. He did not want them either, so I took my two snails and placed them on the plate of the young associate; we then proceeded with our meeting. After the meeting, the associate said he was being replaced by the South Korean Commissioner of Patents, who would be the translator and who was looking forward to meeting me. The Commissioner showed up and sat down with us and we had a nice conversation regarding the Korean patent law and Patent Office. We then got up for our evening entertainment. This entertainment was at a high-end brothel on a street loaded full of brothels. I found it amazing that I was sitting for all practical purposes at a whore house with the Korean Commissioner of Patents, who seemed quite at home there. Anyway, the entertainment there I will not go into, but suffice to say I was happy to leave, although it was a good experience being with the Commissioner of Patents, albeit under unusual circumstances.

I often would go from South Korea to Taiwan, where we had several associates with whom we did business. On my first trip to Taiwan, however, I had no clients to call upon, so I went to the office buildings next to the Taiwanese Patent Office and looked for English-language identification of patent law firms. I found a few and knocked on their doors, being the good shoe salesman that I was. I introduced myself and ultimately developed several good clients in Taiwan. Again, it helped to have big cajónes.

On one occasion, I took Sue and Pam with me. We stayed at a wonderful hotel. I went off to do business and they went to the Chiang Kai-shek Museum. We were warned at the desk of the boutique hotel where we were staying to only get into official cars. Somehow that message did not get through to Sue and Pam because, after they went to the museum, which they enjoyed, they got into an unmarked taxi, which proceeded to take them to some section of Taipei where they were supposed to buy gold and jewelry. Sue took charge and threatened the driver to either return them back to the hotel or she would take necessary action to do whatever she was going to do to him. In any event, her scorn was enough for the driver, who immediately returned them to the hotel.

One of the scarier moments occurred in the Taiwanese airport. In the early 2000's, I had some heart issues that necessitated me getting a single chamber pacemaker. I had to be cautious around electromagnetic fields of the type used in the older airport scanning equipment. Rick Byrne was with me as we entered the Taipei airport. We were in a hurry and I thought I would go through the scanner as opposed to getting in a separate line to be hand patted. I went through the scanner and it dinged. I had forgotten to take off my watch, so I went through it again. This time, it dinged because I had my glasses in a metal case in my pocket. I went through a third time and Rick and I headed to the proper gate. I suddenly felt weak and broke into a cold sweat. I told Rick what was occurring and he later told me all he could think of was who was going to get my body back to Pittsburgh. Meanwhile, I was trying to decide whether I wanted to die in Taipei or get on the plane and die in Seoul. Fortunately, the pacemaker rebooted, the color came back to my face, and all was well thereafter.

One of the most useful techniques I had in developing clients in Asian countries was to invite a young associate from one of the law firms I was visiting to spend the summer in our law firm in Pittsburgh, where we would teach them about US patent law. This worked greatly to our advantage, and almost every summer we had a guest visitor from a foreign law firm. The young lawyers in our office and our staff were always very receptive to these young foreign associates and it left a lasting impression with them and helped to create a solid business relationship. The two earliest young associates were Taka Kitaura from Osaka and Yoon Kim from South Korea. Both remain solid friends of the firm, many years after their internships.

2. European clients

I was also able to develop business relationships with many companies and intellectual property law firms in Europe. I was starting to earn and enjoy the title of "Rainmaker."

Thanks to Bob Oglevee, I had developed an expertise in the area of plants. Ultimately, our law firm was always ranked either 1, 2, or 3 in the number of plant patents issued every year by the United States Patent and Trademark Office. My clients were mostly European plant breeders and so it was always enjoyable to visit them. In Holland, I attended a number of the annual bulb fairs and dealt with many plant breeders there.

One of my favorite European clients in the plant breeding business was Elsner pac Jungpflanzen Gbr, located outside of Dresden, Germany. I visited them on three or four occasions and I always had Sue with me on those trips. Wilhelm Elsner, the founder of that company, had been a prisoner of war in World War II. He spent two years in Texas as a prisoner of war, where he said he was treated better than he had been in his own country. Following World War II, when Germany was split, Dresden became part of East Germany and the communist German Democratic Republic (East German government). The East German government had taken over the Elsner company and became the owners with Wilhelm Elsner simply running the operation but having no ownership interest in it. He continued to develop new varieties of geraniums and these were offered to the Oglevee Company in the United States. I was able to obtain United States plant patents on these varieties from Wilhelm Elsner in exchange for a license agreement that the East German government signed. To obtain this agreement, I needed to send lawyers from Wüsthoff & Wüsthoff in Munich into East Germany to get the signature of the East German government. Under normal circumstances, a plant breeder retains ownership of the plant patent and merely grants a license to use it to those who desire to asexually reproduce and sell that product. However, I was able to convince the East German government to relinquish ownership to Oglevee in the United States, for which we would pay a royalty on every cutting made from the patented variety. This was a huge success and Oglevee, who had fifty percent of the geranium business in the United States, sent huge royalty checks every year to the East German government in exchange for the ability to grow these varieties. When the Berlin Wall came down, ownership was reinstated in Wilhelm Elsner and his family.

After one of my visits, I received a beautiful card from that company, which read as follows.

Dear Russell,

Your name accompanied our company now for almost thirty years. You patented for us seventy plant patents by your law firm since 1983. We say in this way thanks for the very good and close cooperation. We wish for years ahead of you good health and family well being.

Very truly yours,
Andrea Ludwig

Andrea was the daughter of Wilhem Elsner and the letter was signed October 19, 2012.

3. Canadian and Mexican Clients

I also developed wonderful relationships with our neighbors to the north and south. The Canadian companies with which we did business were not unlike the US companies so it was business as usual. I did represent Fernlea Nurseries from Ontario and assisted them in many negotiations with US companies over plant varieties that they were growing through one of their Florida subsidiaries.

In Mexico, I had also developed good business relationships with several Mexican intellectual property law firms. I would meet with them from time to time in the United States but on one occasion, I was on vacation in Zihuantanejo, Mexico and arranged to visit our best Mexican associate in Mexico City. Unfortunately, the day before my meeting in Mexico City, I had eaten oysters on the beach that I purchased from a young Mexican who had collected them. Sue had warned me not do anything that stupid but of course I did. By the time I got to Mexico City, I was sicker than a dog with Montezuma's Revenge and had to call off my meeting with the Mexican associate. I was able to conduct some business with him by phone but I did not do myself any favors by eating those oysters on the beach.

4. Haitian Clients

Perhaps one of the most unusual foreign clients was in Haiti, which I visited on two occasions. The client was Home of Champions in Port-au-Prince, Haiti. They were owned by a gentleman named Jule Tomar. Jule had stopped in Haiti on the way home from Europe following World War II, where he bought some handbags that he took back to New York and New Jersey and sold on the open market. That was very successful so he continued to develop ties in Haiti and ultimately built a huge factory there to manufacture softballs and baseballs for the United States including for many of the professional teams. The technology that he developed over the years with a chemist in his company generally involved the core material found in the centers of the softballs and baseballs.

My first visit to Haiti was with Bob DeMajistre, who had met Jule in New Jersey. Port-au-Prince was the poorest city I had ever been in in my life. I traveled there by myself and met Bob, who traveled in from the Dominican Republic. I waited for him at the airport and, when his airplane landed, there were people leaving the plane with crates on their heads full of chickens and Bob, who was small of stature, got off barely able to breathe after having been jammed in with all the Haitians and chickens. Bob and I visited Jule at his home, which was absolutely gorgeous. It had marble floors and servants and it was an example of the tremendous division between the haves and the have-nots in the country of Haiti. We conducted our business and had an afternoon to kill. We decided we would visit the Barbancourt rum distillery that was at the top of the mountain some seventy-five hundred feet above Port-au-Prince. This rum factory had been the previous home of Papa Doc, the ruler of Haiti for many years. He was succeeded by his son, Baby Doc, and the castle on top of the mountain was turned over to the rum company. Bob and I had an open Jeep and as we drove up the mountain through villages, we passed people carrying automatic weapons standing in the streets. We never turned our heads, but continued to drive up to the top of the mountain. When we got there, we found the beautiful rum factory and proceeded to sample small quantities of the different rums they made. Unfortunately, drinking rum at that elevation can have a temporary inebriating effect. As we drove down the mountain, the men with rifles would stand out to stop us and we never slowed down; we simply kept going to the bottom where we then went to our hotel to clean up for dinner.

Dinner was spent at the Hotel Oloffson, which was the hotel that was the basis for the book *The Comedians*. There was an evening show that Bob and I attended, which was unbelievable. As the only Caucasians, we were put in the front row right next to the stage on which a fire was built in a big wide metal pot. A gorgeous, completely unclothed Haitian woman came out and started doing voodoo dances and proceeded to climb into this pot of burning coals, where a stark-naked young man proceeded to take pieces of burning kindling out of the fire, running it over her body as they both did these incredible dances. To this day, neither Bob nor I can figure out how they pulled this off. I have given up on trying to figure that one out, but it was quite an evening. As we were getting ready to leave Haiti, Bob decided he needed to take back a bunch of Haitian rum from the rum factory we visited. The problem was that he spent most of his money, and we found out we did not have enough to pay the exit tax at the airport. We therefore went over to the casino where they were dealing one-deck blackjack. Fortunately, I had learned how to count cards, particularly from one deck, and I was able to enlarge our fifty-some dollar holding to in excess of one hundred dollars, which enabled us to pay the exit tax and get the heck out of the country.

On my second trip to Haiti, I went by myself and went immediately to the factory where the baseballs and softballs were being produced. When I walked into this huge factory, I thought I must have come at break time because I could see all the women sitting at their tables lifting their arms and then setting them down, then lifting their arms and setting them down again. I thought it was some sort of exercise until I realized what they were doing. In each hand they had needles with threads and they were sewing up the baseballs and softballs and they did this for eight hours on end. I then met with Jule and took care of our patent business regarding his pending US patents. Jule then asked me if I would go down to the government building in Port-au-Prince and talk to this one official and give him some money to obtain certain rights that Jule was trying to acquire in Haiti. It smelled of a bribe to me, so I respectfully declined and he understood and did not hold it against me, but I was happy to get out of the country once again.

5. Russian Clients

When I went on my "Roots" tour with my family, I arranged to meet with a Russian associate in Moscow who was handling business matters for our US clients in Russia. It was a Saturday and he met me in his office. It was very interesting that even in those days, it was clear to me that we would be better off to not be doing business with the Russians.

RUSS AND SUE ON THEIR WEDDING NIGHT, DECEMBER 31, 1960.

RUSS AND SUE A FEW YEARS AGO.

RUSS, SISTER JUDY AND COUSIN FRED AT ZAGARE, LITHUANIA IN 2007 WHERE
8 FAMILIES NAMED ORKIN WERE KILLED BY RUSSIANS IN EARLY 1900S.

RUSS'S FIRST HOME IN GENEVA, OHIO BUILT BY HIS DAD ON
LAND GIVEN TO HIM BY RUSS'S GRANDMOTHER.

RUSS'S HOME IN GENEVA FROM AGE 5 THROUGH HIGH SCHOOL AND COLLEGE.

RUSS AND MR. MATSUI, A JAPANESE PATENT ATTORNEY IN TOKYO IN 1984.

1984

RUSS AND OSAMU KITAMURA, A JAPANESE PATENT ATTORNEY IN OSAKA IN 1984.

RUSS AND MISTERS MCCONNELL AND BRADLEY FROM TAYLOR WILSON
COMPANY IN NEGOTIATIONS WITH JAPANESE COMPANY REPRESENTATIVES
INCLUDING THEIR PRESIDENT IN PITTSBURGH IN LATE 70'S.

RUSS AND JAPANESE PATENT ATTORNEYS AND AGENTS IN
MR. KITAMURA'S OFFICE IN OSAKA IN 1989.

RUSS AND YOON KIM, A YOUNG LAWYER FROM S. KOREA
WORKING ONE SUMMER AT RUSS'S OFFICE.

RUSS AND A JAPANESE PATENT ATTORNEY FROM OSAKA.

RUSS AND PARTNER RICK BYRNE AND A JAPANESE
GEISHA DURING DINNER AT MT. FUJI.

RUSS AND PARTNER JULIE MEDER AND FRANK CALANDRA
AT A JENNMAR CHRISTMAS PARTY.

RUSS, PARTNER BILL LOGSDON AND BOB DEMAJISTRE WITH
LOHMANN GMBH ATTORNEYS AND TECHNICAL EXPERTS ON PLANT
VISIT TO LOHMANN'S FACILITIES IN NEUWIED, GERMANY.

CATTLE DRIVE ON ONLY MAJOR HIGHWAY THROUGH CROW
INDIAN RESERVATION SOUTH OF HARDEN, MONTANA.

FREDDIE AND BRIAN IN FRONT OF UNCLE TOM'S CABIN
AT THE BOULDER RIVER RANCH, MONTANA.

RUSS WITH RAINBOW TROUT CAUGHT ON MISSOURI RIVER AT CRAIG , MONTANA.

RUSS TYING FLYS.

RUSS WITH LARGEMOUTH BASS CAUGHT IN HEAD WATERS LAKE, FELLSMERE, FLORIDA.

RUSS WITH RED FISH CAUGHT IN BAFFIN BAY, TEXAS.

RUSS, ANDY, ANDY'S DAD BRUCE, EX-SON-IN-LAW
STEVE, GRANDSON MATT, FRIEND LOU KUSHNER AND DAVID HILL
AT AYAKULIK RIVER CAMP ON KODIAK ISLAND. ALASKA.

RUSS AND BRIAN WITH 183 POUND HALIBUT FROM THE OCEAN OFF KODIAK ISLAND.

RUSS WITH RECORD NORTHERN PIKE, 471/2 INCHES, 30 POUNDS CAUGHT AT VIEW POSTE CAMP, LAKE MISTASSINI, QUEBEC.

RUSS ACTING GOOFY WITH A LARGE LAKE MISTASSINI PIKE.

RUSS ON PORTAGE IN THE WATERSHED OF LAKE MISTASSINI.

TIP – THE MORNING AFTER THE NIGHT FROM HELL, TRES MARIAS, MEXICO.

RUSS, DENNY SLEVIN AND GUIDE CHARLIE ISERHOFF PREPARING
FOR A 1 WEEK RIVER RUN OFF OF LAKE MISTASSINI.

RUSS WITH 20 POUND PERMIT CAUGHT AT CASA BLANCA, ASCENSION BAY, MEXICO.

GUIDE WITH 63 POUND CUBERA SNAPPER CAUGHT BY FREDDIE
AT CLUB PACIFICO, ISLA DE COIBA, PANAMA.

RUSS WITH 212 POUND BLACK MARLIN CAUGHT AT CLUB PACIFICO.

RUSS WITH 40 POUND BLUE TREVALLY CAUGHT IN THE SEYCHELLES IN 2014.

RUSS AND TOM WITH SEYCHELLES BONEFISH.

GRANDSON WILL WITH A NICE SAILFISH CAUGHT OFF
THE COAST OF COSTA RICA IN 2010.

FAMILY TYES AT NATIONAL CASTING CALL IN WASHINGTON D.C.

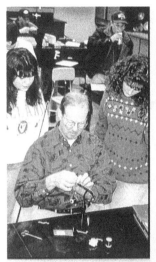

Jack Bogut — the student

"Three of life's great pleasures are to learn, to share — and to teach. The Baldwin High School Fly Fishing Club, "Family Tyes," does this so well.

Paul Hindes and Chuck McKinney teach these young people how to do something that they will enjoy for the rest of their lives. They, in turn, share the love of something discovered with their families and friends and ultimately teach others and pass the gift along. That's a lot of what living a good life is all about, isn't it?

And these young people are learning it at a very early age. What a leg up!"

Jack Bogut.

LOCAL PITTSBURGH RADIO HOST TYING FLYS AT FAMILY TYES FLY TYING NIGHT AT BALDWIN HIGH SCHOOL.

SUE AND CHILDREN ON A RAFTING TRIP ON GREEN RIVER IN UTAH IN 1981.

18 YEARS OF YOGA HELPS!

THREE GENERATIONS OF ORKIN'S FISHING THE MISSOURI SEPTEMBER 2023.

BEN AND MIKEY AT SWEETGRASS RANCH IN 2008.

Chapter IX

Full-time Fisherman

A. The Grouse Hunter?

Let me pause before getting into the meat of this book to discuss my prowess or, more accurately, my lack of prowess as a grouse hunter.

When I moved to Pittsburgh in 1967, there was a good population of both grouse and pheasant in Western Pennsylvania. The ruffed grouse is the state bird of Pennsylvania.

We lived next to the old Allegheny County work farm, which first received inmates in 1869, and officially closed in 1971. The property was gradually converted into the Regional Industrial Development Corporation (RIDC) Industrial Park. In 1967, the land was full of old apple trees, blackberries, other fruit trees and vines, and pheasants. You could hear them clucking every night and they continually raided my tomato plants. Someone told me to put mothballs around the plants to keep the pheasants away, but my tomato pasta tasted like mothballs so I learned to live with the pheasants. Eventually, they disappeared throughout Western Pennsylvania because of loss of habitat, etc. and, more importantly, because of the West Nile virus.

The grouse population was good in the late 1960's and 1970's, and I became a grouse hunter. I never owned a new shotgun, but I had my dad's Double Barrel Stevens 12 gauge, which I never shot and, over time, I purchased a used 20-gauge pump and a 12-gauge semi-automatic. My fishing buddy Bill Hill has a pacifist in his family, so he gave me his over/under 16 gauge. I eventually gave all my guns to Brian and one of my grandsons, so I remain gunless.

There were two grouse hunting seasons in Pennsylvania, one in the fall and the other in the winter through early January. The fall season was known as the hunting season because the woods were full of crunchy leaves and the grouse could hear you coming from a mile away and they shot out way ahead of you. The winter season was known as the killing season because the grouse hunkered down in the snow and the dogs could easily go on point until you arrived. For me, the winter season was also the hunting season because I was a terrible shot so it did not matter whether the grouse were hunkered down or not.

The terrain in Western Pennsylvania for game was very severe. It consists of hills and valleys covered with briars and other physical impediments. Abandoned strip mines were a little easier, but the grouse always seemed to find a briar patch in which to hide.

I had three sets of hunting buddies. First and foremost was my neighbor and good friend Freddie Smith, the local orthodontist. He always had a brown Labrador retriever for hunting, but none of his dogs were very good. It was more likely that you would trip over the dog than the dog would find a grouse. On rare occasions, the dog would find a bird and one of us would take a lucky shot and get it. We would then immediately quit the hunt and hurry to the closest convenience store to buy the dog a hot dog for its efforts. Freddie would then time how long it took the dog to eat the hot dog; the record was under ten seconds. Freddie and I would then head to our favorite bar in the middle of the boondocks where, in the fall, we would have a couple of beers and, in the winter, a couple of shots to warm our bodies. The problem was the female bartender in this bar was young and had terrible teeth. Freddie tipped her more money to fix her teeth than what it cost for our food and beverages.

On one occasion, we were hunting without his dog. Our favorite spot was a briar patch a couple hundred yards or so long along an old strip mine. Since we had no dog and Freddie was a better shot, I told him to go to the end of the patch and be ready as I would crawl through the patch and kick the grouse out the patch end for him to shoot. I gave Freddie time to get to the patch end. I started crawling through the patch on my hands and knees. It was a tough crawl but it was a good day, and I could hear the grouse flushing out in front of me. Unfortunately, I could not hear any shots from Freddie. Finally, when I got to the end of the patch, I saw Freddie's gun and my gun leaning against a tree and Freddie was sitting under a tree building a fire, which he loved to do. He was so into it that he failed to hear or see the whole flock of grouse I had proceeded to flush.

Occasionally, Bob Brasso would go with Freddie and me. He oversaw all weapons for the County Police, and he really knew what he was doing. He trained me on all safety aspects of hunting in the woods, and I remain eternally grateful since I was very comfortable with a gun, albeit not able to hit my birds.

I once saw Bob standing in front of a brush pile taking a leak when a grouse flushed from the very brush pile. He casually lifted his 20 gauge with one hand and shot the bird without ever interrupting his leak. That is a skill.

The second group of grouse hunters was two young men, Walter and Peter, who both had good dogs and knew what they were doing. I would occasionally get a bird with my 12 gauge when hunting with them, but they shamed me into using my 20 gauge so my success rate dropped appreciably.

They were very protective of their hunting spots and, on one occasion when we got into semi-familiar territory, Walter stopped the truck and put a blindfold on me. He drove the truck in circles until I was completely confused on direction. These boys were always good for a laugh.

Walter would bring two dogs, which he kept at a trainer, Blitz and a young dog who was in training. Blitz tended to take off far ahead, so Walter had Blitz on an electric collar, which he used frequently. By the end of the day, Blitz looked more like a french fry than a bird dog. On another occasion after Blitz worked the morning, Walter brought out the young dog for the afternoon hunt. The first thing the young dog did was to put his nose in a porcupine hole and the rest of the day was spent at the vet, who carefully removed many porcupine quills from the nose of the poor dog.

The third hunting group consisted of Walter (in his 40's), me (in my 60's), and Rupert Friday (in his 80's). How is that for a range of ages, all interested in spending time in the woods hunting the state bird? Rupert raised hunting dogs and was a true expert in that and at hunting grouse. He was limited by his age, so we primarily hunted in old strip mines where it was not difficult to navigate. On one occasion, Rupert's dog took off after Blitz and somehow got lost. Rupert, who was a retired physician and a kind and gentle man, went livid. We never did find his dog that day but, the next day, a farmer called him with the dog in hand and all was well.

My grouse hunting days ended when I had a pacemaker inserted in the area of the shoulder where a gun would normally rest. It still was one of the best periods of my life. With the local fishing season over, I had the woods of Pennsylvania calling.

B. The Transition

When did I give away all my spinning rods (except one heavy rod for barracuda) to my grandkids and start buying fly rods? When did bobbers become strike indicators? When did I transition from a meat fisherman to a sports fisherman? It all happened in the first couple of years following our move to Pittsburgh. It happened when I became a trout fisherman.

Thanks to friends, John Shallenberger, Tad Potter, and Bill Hill, all native Pittsburghers and avid trout fishermen from those starting days.

John used a fly rod with minnows on a Joe's fly to catch trout in the many streams of Western Pennsylvania. Tad and Bill were more sophisticated. They got me started on salmon eggs in North-Central Pennsylvania and soon I was a pretty good nymph fisherman. Still no need to cast a fly line any distance at all. Over time, I learned to fly cast and by the early 1970's, I could handle most streams in the Grand Canyon of Pennsylvania.

C. Pennsylvania and surrounds

1. Western Pennsylvania

My fishing in Western Pennsylvania started as previously stated with John Shallenberger fishing the little streams surrounding the Kittanning area, namely the South Fork of Pine and Scrubgrass Creek in Goheenville, Pennsylvania. Both streams were tiny, several yards across, and we fished them with hip boots and minnows on a Joe's fly. As the spring season for trout ended, we fished the Allegheny River in John's small Grumman Square Back Canoe with a 6 HP motor. We fished above Parker for smallmouth bass. Initially we used artificial bait, but there were many wonderful ruffles and before long we were both fishing with fly rods and various types of streamers. In the late fall and early winter, we fished at Mosgrove, which is just north of Kittanning on the Allegheny River, for walleyes. We would start fishing about an hour before dark when the walleye hitting was best. As soon as the mud puppies started to take our bait, we knew it was time to quit. The mud puppy is a member of the salamander family and has legs and is about twelve inches long. It scurries along the bottom, eating everything in sight.

Circa 1980, my buddies and I decided we needed a father-son fishing trip or two. The group included Denny Slevin and Buzzy Lodge from Pittsburgh, Tip Davidson and Keith Helfer from Columbus, and me, together with all our sons. The first one was an overnight camping trip to the Youghiogheny River at Confluence, Pennsylvania. The "Yough" as it is called is a one-hundred-thirty-four-mile stretch of water that runs through West Virginia, Maryland, and Pennsylvania. It is a Lenape word meaning "a stream flowing in a contrary direction." Confluence is about ten miles south of Ohiopyle, the best-known white-water rafting river in Pennsylvania. There is a good-sized dam there with an out flow that is full of fish including trout. We camped along the shore and the boys started fishing with artificial lures and worms. They were not having much luck so I decided to go to the local bait store in Confluence and get some mealworms. The adults went with me and we left Keith's son in charge since he was the oldest, all of eleven or twelve. We got the mealworms and stopped for that famous "just one beer." There was a pool table in the bar and we had a heated game of pool and a few more beers. By the time we got back, only two or three of the kids had fallen in but they apparently had a good time in our absence. Using the mealworms, the boys started catching fish and all was well.

The overnight went well, with the practical joker Tip putting some sort of turtle in my sleeping bag. The group got a kick out of me scrambling to extricate myself from the sleeping bag. Fortunately, it was not a snapping turtle.

The next morning, we took off for Cucumber Falls at Ohiopyle, where we were going to do some hiking. Brian somehow fell in and got his shoes soaking wet. Buzzy had an extra pair of tennis shoes so he gave the shoes to Brian. Brian proceeded to trip and bang up his knee because the shoes were too big. Fast forward to the next week and a parent's night at Brian's grade school. A number of parents were standing in front of the bulletin board where the kids had posted their written stories. Brian had written about our camping trip. He explained his fall as follows: "Mr. Lodge lent me his extra pair of tennis shoes. They were too big and I tripped and fell, scraping my knee. I started to cry but my dad gave me some Red Man to chew and told me I would be fine." Needless to say, I left the bulletin board as fast as I could before anyone could figure out that I was that dad.

2. *Central Pennsylvania*

I started fishing Central Pennsylvania shortly after arriving in Pittsburgh. The primary location was Pine Creek, located in the Grand Canyon of Pennsylvania. We always stayed at the Cedar Run Inn, which was an old hotel located on Pine Creek. We fished the entire Kettle Creek area, which included Kettle Creek, the Germania Branch of Kettle Creek, Cross Fork, Slate Run, and Young Woman's Creek. We always fished opening day, which was April 15, so very often it was cold and sometimes even snowing. The Cedar Run Inn was an old hotel that had been around forever. When we first started going, it was owned by a little old lady named Lulu Johnson, who charged us twelve dollars per night and that included two meals and a place to sleep. If you drank the milk she served at dinner, you got dessert; if you did not drink your milk, no dessert. Lulu was a great little character and, on opening day, her older sister from Buffalo, who worked in the post office, would take time off and come to help her run the inn.

On Saturday night, we would go to the Wagon Wheel Bar in Cammal, Pennsylvania, which was only a few miles from Cedar Run. It was a crazy place with all the locals dancing and singing and having a good time. On one occasion, there was a rock-and-roll group playing the songs of the day. A local went into the bathroom, took off all his clothes, wrapped himself in toilet paper, came out on the dance floor, and started dancing to the music. The toilet paper slowly came off and, before long, he was dancing naked on the dance floor. The place went nuts!

Before the second year of traveling to Cedar Run, I called my friend Tip in Columbus and told him he ought to join us. Tip was a practical joker and it was always tough to get even with him for the many jokes he pulled on all his friends. This time I got him good. I told him that the Cedar Run Inn was run by this beautiful young lady named Lulu Johnson and that there were good times to be had and that he should call her and make arrangements to join us for the coming season. He made that call to Lulu and told her that he understood that there were good times to be had at the Cedar Run Inn, thinking all along that he was talking with this sweet young lady. Lulu listened to him and this is what she said, "Young man, we have as many good times as we have good timers," but she welcomed him to the Cedar Run Inn on opening day. When he arrived, he was shocked to see this 4'11" woman who came up to his waist since he is about 6'5". After a few years, Lulu sold the Cedar Run Inn to Peggy and Randy from New York City. They were upscale young people and they turned the Cedar Run Inn into a beautiful old hotel resort. There was classical music at night and while Randy ran the kitchen, Peggy ran the hotel and attempted to clamp down on any activities of our crazy group.

The fishing was great on all the above-mentioned streams and a number of the areas were fly fishing only, which suited us. One time we were fishing on Cross Fork Stream when it started to snow very heavily. I was standing in the middle of the stream fishing with my buddy Tip on one side of me and Keith on the other side. It was getting colder and colder and the snow was getting heavier and heavier as we stood in the middle of the stream staring at each other. To the rescue came Tip, who reached inside his waders and pulled out a bottle of scotch. We then proceeded to work on that bottle while we laughed and carried on in the middle of the stream with fish all around us and snow coming down harder all the time. When we finished the bottle, we headed to the local tavern which was called The Cross Fork Tavern. The parking lot was full of pickup trucks owned by the locals and there were hound dogs in the back of virtually every one of the trucks. We got out and walked into the tavern, but Keith stayed behind. Keith started howling at the top of his lungs, sounding very much like a hound dog. Immediately, all the hound dogs in the parking lot started howling back at him and it was quite a scene until the locals in the bar heard what was going on and came running out to save their dogs from whatever it was that was causing the problem. The locals were not very happy with us, but after we bought a few rounds, we all became friends and life went on as usual.

On the way to the Grand Canyon, we always stopped at Big Fishing Creek, which was one of our favorite fishing spots in Lamar, Pennsylvania. The stream was well-loaded with native and stocked fish, but they were very difficult to catch. There were occasional hatches and if you caught the hatches right, you were able to land some beauties. Tad Potter had known about Big Fishing Creek and he was the one that initially took us there. One time we were fishing and fishing got slow, and suddenly we could not figure out where Tad was; he was missing. Tad, always known for his tremendous appetite had, unbeknownst to us, gone into Lamar and found a Kentucky Fried Chicken. He arrived back on the stream with buckets of chicken and mashed potatoes and, while we chastised him for buying way too much food, we all enjoyed the feast that day.

3. Lakes

My old partner Demo and I used to chat during work hours about fishing. On one occasion, we decided to skip working that afternoon and go fishing. The doctor down the hall from our office had a place on a small lake in Northwestern Pennsylvania, and had invited me to fish it any time. Bob ran home and packed up his fishing gear, a six-pack or two, and some cheese he had buried in his back yard. I ran home and got my fishing gear and borrowed Don Lampus's canoe, and off we went.

Demo was about 5'2" and, after a while of fishing, he stood up to do his casting. I never saw anyone stand up in a canoe and, sure enough, after a few minutes he fell overboard. He was going to try to climb in and I had visions of going in as well. I talked him out of it and dragged his sorry body to shore so we could sip a beer, cut the cheese, and head on home.

On another occasion, we decided that our young sons needed the experience of ice fishing. One Saturday in mid-winter, we headed for Put-in-Bay, Ohio with our two sons. Bob had also invited a state highway patrol friend to go along, which I thought was a great idea because if Demo and I had a beer or two, he could drive.

It was a cold, miserable day and we flew to Put-in-Bay Island from the mainland on a small Sea King-type plane. The outfitter, who had arranged our trip, took us out to our tent-like structure on Lake Erie by snowmobile. The wind was howling and it was getting colder by the minute. We caught a few perch and threw them outside the tent since we were all cramped for space. At one point, the tent flaps broke away from the two-by-four tent posts. We pounded the nails back in using a frozen perch as the hammer. The conditions were so rough that the outfitter had to come get us in an old Beaver de Havilland aircraft, which was far more reliable in bad weather than the Sea King-type aircraft we came in on.

The only beer that was consumed was by the highway patrolman, so Demo and I had to drive back to Pittsburgh.

That was my first and last ice fishing adventure.

D. Montana

I started fishing Montana in the late 1970's. Tad's brother Tom and Bill had traveled to Montana in Tad's big Winnebago RV and had discovered the Boulder River Ranch, which ran along the Boulder River in Southeastern Montana. It was owned by Gil Aller and his wife Eleanor, along with his son Steve and daughter-in-law Jean. Steve was a falconer and we often watched him feed and work the birds in the evenings. Jean was the businessperson of the family, particularly when Gil got a little long in the tooth. The ranch was basically a working dude ranch and most of the guests were there for horseback riding and other ranch activities. Our group was often the only group of fishermen. There were many horses and Steve and Jean's daughter Jordan was Miss Montana, Rodeo. There was about a mile of stream from above a waterfall that was loaded with good-sized rainbows. There were some native brook trout but, under strict instructions from Gil, we kept them and the cook would fry them for breakfast. Gil advised that the "brookies" ate the rainbow spawn and he wanted to keep the brookie population at a minimum.

There was a main lodge and dining room centrally located on the property, but we always stayed in "Uncle Tom's" cabin located at the far end of the property. Fishing was always excellent with dry flies to match the hatch and grasshoppers being preferred. The cows would walk along the stream kicking up grasshoppers, which would land on the water. Follow the cows, and grasshopper fishing was great.

Every year or so, Freddie and I would drive to the end of the dirt road where the ranch was located. The road ended at a box canyon, and the East Boulder Branch flowed down the mountain into the main Boulder River. The East Boulder ran steeply down a rocky shoreline, forming numerous pools and small waterfalls. There were often cutthroats in the pools and under the waterfalls, but they were difficult to get to because of the terrain. Freddie and I would split up and fish alternate pools. It was great fun, but a tad on the dangerous side. Any fly that floated seemed to work. We were forever hanging up on tree limbs so the fish that we caught were not large but were well worth it. A half day of that fishing left us exhausted and satisfied.

On one occasion, the entire group headed to the box canyon to fish both the East Branch and West Branch of the Boulder River. It was a bit of a hike but well worth it. As we trekked over a hilly trail, we ran into a fish game warden. Not a single one of us had our Montana fishing license with us. I managed to talk our way out of a ticket on the promise we would make copies of our licenses and forward them to the warden's office. We all complied and thereafter carried our fishing licenses whenever we left the ranch.

The ranch next to the Boulder River Ranch was called Boulder's Meadow and was owned by the Levi Strauss family. Freddie got to know the ranch manager, who let us fish the river on their property. There was a monster rainbow trout under a small bridge, but no one could catch it. The ranch manager had named the fish, but I cannot remember the name. For purposes of this story, I will call him Louie.

Freddie and I devised a plan to catch Louie, and it worked. I snuck down to the edge of the river next to the bridge with a huge grasshopper fly. Freddie caught a bunch of live grasshoppers and threw them off the bridge one at a time. Louie gobbled up every one. I then cast my hopper fly and Louie took it, hook, line, and sinker. Louie was a beauty and we carefully took his picture and released him. The ranch manager could not believe that we caught Louie, but was pleased that we released him unharmed. We did not tell him how we did it.

In the evenings, we would fish tricos until dark and then head up the road to the Roadkill Café for a nightcap and bumper pool. The slogan of the bar, which appeared in bold letters, was "From Your Grill to Ours." The Roadkill Café was a hoot and a favorite to all. The Café was often frequented by famous people, but I did not recognize any of them.

One year, Freddie and I decided to take Brian and go to the Sweetgrass County Fair. We were trying to get Brian, who was sixteen, to talk to the many young cowgirls. He wanted no part of that because they had hairy armpits. A bull got loose and came roaring down the midway and all three of us jumped in the back of a pickup truck as the bull roared by. We left after that.

Our group started fishing the Bighorn River in 1984. The Bighorn was opened in 1981 and it was loaded with huge trout and other species. We usually tied this trip in with our trip to the ranch. Initially, we stayed in Fort Smith, where the Bighorn Dam was located. We stayed in one of the few motels and ate at Polly's Restaurant, which only served a couple of things for dinner. All I remember is night after night of meatloaf.

Our principal guide on the Bighorn was George Kelly who, after a year or two, built a beautiful little lodge called Kingfisher Lodge, and that is where we stayed thereafter.

We also fished the famous Spring Creeks in the Livingston area. They are the Armstrongs, DePuys, and Nelsons. All three have substantial trout populations, but they are very hard to catch even though there are a limited number of fishermen. Large portions of the land is privately owned and a fee is charged to fish those properties. Under Montana law, the fishermen have the right to be in the water but not the right to be on private property around the Spring Creeks. Because the fishing was difficult, we usually hired John Green, a top fishing guide, to help us pick the fly to match the hatch. More often than not, we were successful with him along.

One time, Tad and I fished Armstrongs without a guide. With fish rising all around us, I only caught one trout and Tad did not catch any, although he tried every fly in his many fly boxes. Later that night, we learned that the fish were taking a small cream-colored emerger. Oh well, we will get them next time.

We also fished a private lake on a ranch in the Crazy Mountains. We had met Bob Bergquest, a Montana guide, while fishing the Bighorn. Bob took Bill and me to a very nice lake that was well-stocked with rainbows and a couple of other cross-breeds with the rainbows. The first year we fished the lake, there were grasshoppers everywhere and we each caught many fish, some of which were trophy sized. The second and final year on the lake, we caught next to nothing. The adjacent ranch owner had planted a crop of sunflowers and the pesticide he used killed all the grasshoppers. Where were the environmentalists when we needed them?

The last seven years, I fished the Missouri with Beau Strathman, a guide I had met in the Bahamas and who resides on the Missouri north of the Holter Dam. The first few years I fished with Bill. Bill and I would fish the Bighorn for three days and then cross country to the Missouri. We did not like traveling on the expressways, so we tended to take the back roads and enjoy the scenery. On one occasion, we chose to cut across a huge Crow Indian reservation. There was only one paved road to take. Unfortunately, we picked the day the Crows were having their annual cattle drive in which they rounded up all their cattle and drove them down the highway. There had to be a herd of five hundred or more cattle on the road ahead of us. There were about a dozen or so young Indians controlling the herd. One of them was a young lady who rode up to our vehicle. I asked her how we could get around the herd. She politely told us that if we just drive slowly right up to the herd, it would spread out and we could go right through. It absolutely worked and we were on our way.

The following year, Bill and I again took off cross country from Fort Smith to the Missouri. This time, we got completely lost. We knew if we went north, we would get to the Yellowstone River and Route 90. We came to a dirt road heading north and we took it. In a short time, we knew we were in trouble because the road narrowed and there were grass and flowers growing in the middle of the road. That is when we got our flat tire. It took us fifteen minutes to find the spare, which was located under the back seat rather than under the rear floor panel. It also took a while to find the jack as well. I had recently had my prostate removed and Bill had had shoulder surgery. Neither of us were supposed to lift anything heavy. Together, we lifted the tire and jacked up the car until we could jointly change the tire. We ultimately found our way to Big Timber and the gas station owner walked down the highway to a used tire store and came back with the identical replacement tire. Every subsequent time we pass through Big Timber, we would stop at that gas station and buy gas, whether we needed it or not.

The last several times, I fished with Brian and my grandson Sam. We took Sam with us when he was only eleven years old. Beau went out of his way to teach Sam the rudiments of fly fishing on the Missouri. The first year Sam was with us, I was fishing with him and Beau when a storm arose. We headed to the boat landing in Craig, which is a fishing town with three fly shops, one restaurant, and two bars. I took Sam into the scuzziest of the bars, where he and I shot pool until Brian showed up. I had a couple of Yukon Jacks while the old lady bartender made Sam a couple of hot chocolates. Sam said his dad had given him ten dollars, which he had in his pocket, so he ended up buying the second round. After Brian showed up, I stood in the parking lot with tears in my eyes, thinking how lucky I was to be fishing in Montana with my son and grandson. Maybe it was the Yukon Jack that made me melancholy.

Brian and Sam now take the middle day of our three-day fishing trip and go bird hunting. They always manage to shoot a few grouse, which Beau so graciously cooks for us along with backstrap from a deer or elk he had previously shot.

Anyone who has spent time in Montana for many years has a horse story or two. I actually have three.

Our group that fished the Bolder River Branch were all avid fishermen. On occasion, Freddie and I and sometimes Don Lampus would take a half day off from fishing and go horseback riding. Tad and Bill would stick with fishing. The head wrangler at the ranch was a young cowgirl named Whister. One afternoon, Whister took Freddie and me, along with a couple of other guests, on a horse ride. I noticed Tad and Bill in the stream at the far end of the ranch. I thought it would be great to ride through the stream where they were fishing and cause them some grief. I went charging down the sand dune toward the stream when the horse fell and landed on my leg. I got my leg out from under the horse, but it hurt like hell. After everyone checked me out to make sure I was okay, we continued our ride. We were close to the station wagon that Tad and Bill had driven to the end of the ranch. I knew they had a cooler of beer, so I talked Whister into riding to the car where we all partook of a beer or two. We then headed back to the ranch with a beer in hand singing cowboy songs. Whister got into all kinds of trouble with Gill because the saddle blankets were all wet from riding back and forth across the stream. Also, he did not like the idea of the guests drinking beer on a horse ride. I know it is against the law to drink and drive a car, but I did not know it applied to horseback.

My second horse story is a "feel good" story. I had always wanted to take my whole family to the ranch once the grandkids were old enough to ride horses. Unfortunately, when that time came, the ranch had been sold to an agglomerate of well-known people, many of whom already owned land along the west Boulder Valley. I believe there were ten in that group, which included Tom Brokaw, John McGuane (the author), and Michael Keaton (the actor) who was from Pittsburgh. The rumor was that the ranch sold for seventy-five million. The new owners cut down all activities and the ranch became another privately owned ranch where outsiders were not welcome and considered trespassers. When my good friend Tad passed away, he had requested that his ashes be spread in the stream at the Boulder River Ranch. His wife Jean and their children, led by Jean's son-in-law Pete, walked into the stream above the ranch and walked to Tad's favorite fishing hole, where they spread his ashes as requested.

After the sale of the ranch, Jean Aller opened a craft shop in Big Timber and Bill and I stopped on our next trip to Montana to say hello. I told her how disappointed I was not to have been able to take our whole family to the ranch. She recommended the Sweetgrass Ranch in Melville, Montana. We signed up for the next year (2008) and Sue and I; Jill and Steve and their three children (Mikey was the youngest at six years old); Pam and Andy and their two boys headed for the Crazy Mountains where the ranch was located. It was a wonderful dude ranch and the kids rode every day. There was a beautiful little mountain stream full of pools of cutthroats. Each day I would take a different grandchild, get on our horses, and head up the mountain to fish the stream. There were a half dozen or so cutthroat in every pool and, if you were careful, you could catch every one. When I ran out of grandchildren to fish with, Sue went along and read a book while I fished. Everyone enjoyed that vacation and still talk about it.

The third horse story was a real adventure. My friend Lee had a cousin named Sarah Schoales who owned the Circle Bar Ranch in the Judith Mountain Range of Montana. I arranged to do a trip to that ranch and then a six-and-a-half-hour horseback ride up the mountain to a little camp built by the ranch on federal grazing lands. She had her cattle on the federal grazing lands at that time.

This trip included me, Tip, my Pittsburgh friend Ray Tarasi and his son Rayme, and John Shallenberger and his boys. John was the elder statesman and he had reservations about riding a horse for six and a half hours. Somebody told him he should wear women's pantyhose and that would lessen the pain. When we lined up at the ranch to get our horses, someone told Sarah that John had pantyhose on and that cracked her up. Her top ranch hand Dean and one other wrangler accompanied us. There was one notoriously semi-wild horse among the horses. We all decided Rayme, who had just graduated from Penn State and was the Nittany Lions' place kicker, was the best athlete and therefore the best choice for the semi-wild horse. Tip, who is not big on heights, decided to bypass the horse ride and go up in the pickup truck to deliver our essentials.

We started up the mountain on horseback and all was going well until we hit an open range leading into a heavily wooded area along a steep cliff. Rayme's horse took off at full speed toward the wooded area and cliff. He was hanging on for dear life. Dean, who had taken Sarah's personal horse, took off after Rayme and got him just before he hit the wooded cliff area. It was like a cowboy catching the runaway stage in an old cowboy movie. Dean changed horses with Rayme so Rayme got Sarah's horse and Dean spent the week on the wild one.

The camp had everything to offer. Those who wanted to fish had plenty of mountain stream. I fell into that group. Those who wanted to ride horses could go out with the two cowboys and mend fences and look after cattle. Those that wanted to hike and climb mountains could do so.

Every morning, Dean would line us up and say it was time to brush our teeth. He would then pass around a bottle of peppermint Schnapps with which to wash our mouth. The evening drink was another Dean special called Orangutang. It was vodka and tang combined. Good for the mountains but not your everyday drink. The food was wonderful with huge steaks cooked on an open fire almost every night.

Rayme had brought along a couple of footballs because he had a tryout with the Cleveland Browns when we returned. Every evening, he would practice with Dean seventy-five yards away and the other cowhand halfway between Dean and Rayme. Rayme would kick the football, Dean would catch it, and throw it to the cowhand, who would return it to Rayme for the next kick. At seven-to eight thousand feet above sea level, the football went a long way. I think this was the high-light of the trip for Dean and the wrangler.

Great trip but one six-and-a-half-hour ride on horseback along a narrow trail up a mountain is enough for me.

I am already looking forward to this year's fishing trip to Montana.

E. Florida

I have enjoyed a wide variety of fishing in Florida. The strangest was a thirty-minute fishing adventure in the Florida Keys as follows.

Demo, my one-time law partner, left the firm in 1984, but we continued to stay in touch. We, along with our wives, went to sailing school in Annapolis. After getting our sailing certificate, we decided to bare boat the lower coast of Florida to Key West. We made the necessary arrangements and picked our boat up at Treasure Harbor on Plantation Key. It was ten o'clock in the morning and the boat owner was already drinking whiskey with his wife or lady friend, and that should have been the first clue. Unbeknownst to us, the boat had been rented to some college kids on spring break the week before and they had left the line on the roller furl for the main sail all tangled up.

We worked our way from the Harbor along the Intercoastal Waterway and then into the wide-open ocean. Before we left Treasure Harbor, Demo had removed whatever flag we were flying and replaced it with a big, long pepperoni stick in honor of his Italian heritage. I was doing most of the sailing (my forte) and Demo was doing most of the navigating (his forte). The first night, we were a long way from any civilization, so we anchored the boat off shore in an uninhabited area on some key that we could not identify. We had intended to eat at some marina of our choice, but none was in sight. Now the fishing connection.

I had a small collapsible fishing rod with me and a few artificial bait. There was a smaller rubber raft on board, so we blew it up and I took off by paddle on the raft to catch our dinner. It did not take long for me to hear an air hiss, telling me that the raft was leaking air. I somehow caught a half dozen or so grunts and headed back to our sailboat. I made it before I sunk to find that Demo had started a charcoal grill, lowered our pepperoni flag, and had sliced it into pieces that he was cooking on our grill. I threw our grunts on and grilled them, and we proceeded to have grunt and pepperoni for dinner.

If that was not enough, the next day we were sailing toward Key West when we figured out we could not lower the main sail because the line was all tangled deep down in the roller furl. We were close to Key West so we pulled into a marina on Stock Island, yelling all the way that we were out of control. Some friendly boatman caught a line we had thrown toward the dock and was able to cleat us off and stop our advance. After getting someone to untangle our line, we proceeded on to Key West. We had the foresight to arrange for the whiskey-drinking boat owner to drive our car to Key West, so we then drove to Miami and the boat owner sailed his boat back to Treasure Harbor.

Another adventure involved tarpon fishing off Islamorada in the Keys. Brian had found a beautiful little boutique beach hotel in Islamorada called Casa Marada. Our whole adult family, Sue and I and our three adult children and their spouses, all met at Casa Marada a few years in the early 2000's. We had a guide from West Virginia who got along famously with Brian. Unfortunately, we got very few tarpon hookups and we started to give him the nickname "No Fish." One night, we were all having dinner and discussing "No Fish." An old guide from the 1960's was sitting at the next table listening to our tales of woe. He had long straggly hair, a beard, gold chains, and tattoos, and he fit the perfect description of a hippy. He told us that if we would meet him under the railroad bridge at eight o'clock that night, he would get us some tarpon. This was immediately bought into by Brian, Pam and her husband Andy, and me. At the designated hour, we met our guide and headed into the bayside of the railroad bridge. Using live crab for bait and heavy spinning gear, we started catching tarpon after tarpon, all good size. Suddenly Pam hooked up with a monster tarpon that she could not handle. I reached over and helped her hold the rod while she tried to bring in line. The tarpon took off and went into the ocean side of the railroad bridge. The bridge is constructed of a series of connected arches, so our guide had to sort of guess which arch the tarpon went through so we could follow it. There was a nasty current and we went through the arch in the dark. The boat scraped the concrete arch, which did not please our heretofore happy guide. On the ocean side, we (my daughter and I) continued to fight the monster tarpon. My arm was getting sore holding the rod and was starting to cramp up. I looked to see where Brian and Andy were, and they were in the back of the boat drinking beer and cheering us on. We ultimately landed the tarpon, which was estimated by the guide to be well in excess of a hundred pounds and, after removing a scale, returned it back into the water slightly tired but none the worse for wear.

Brian and I and other friends who joined me from time to time in tarpon season never had many good catching days but always great fishing days and, after all, that is what it is always about.

I did figure out how to change fishing days into catching days. We would take the middle day of our three-day stay at the Keys and travel by boat into the Everglades, where catching was bountiful. On one occasion, there were so many bull sharks around our boat eating everything we caught that we had to go deeper into the mangroves where we only had to deal with gators. The bird life alone makes a trip into the Everglades worthwhile and catching snook, mangrove snapper, and an occasional red is only a bonus.

For twenty years, we spent our winter in the desert in California. When Covid-19 hit, we had a time getting back to Pittsburgh. Also, we were not able to do the physical hiking and biking we were used to doing. Wake up call, so we have spent the last three winters in Florida, where many of our friends go. We have been spending two months in Vero Beach and one month on Marco Island.

In Vero, we have wonderful friends, the Schmidts. Gordon Schmidt is an avid fisherman and he joined me in the Keys on one occasion. Gordon has an arrangement with a guide, Bobby Fletcher, a native Floridian to fish every Thursday in the ocean, weather permitting. If the wind is up, making ocean fishing impossible, I go with them pulling Bobby's bass boat to the inland lakes west of Vero Beach, for largemouth bass fishing. There are wonderful bodies of water and include Blue Cypress Lake, Headwaters Lake, Stick Marsh Lake, and Kenansville. The later three lakes were built by Florida Fish and Game. Stick Marsh is a sixty-five-hundred-acre impoundment full of structure and home to tournament-size largemouth bass. It was created in 1987 and opened to the public in 1991. Headwaters is a new impoundment in Fellsmere, Florida, and is a ten-thousand-acre lake made in the Indian River area. Kenansville Lake is a shallow twenty-five-hundred-acre impoundment and was a cattle pasture prior to it flooding in 1993. Blue Cypress Lake is the largest lake in Indian County and is a ten-square-mile lake with bountiful birdlife.

I took Pam with Bobby and me and spent a day on Blue Cypress. The first three hours were spent slowly cruising and we were totally mesmerized by the cypress trees and the bird population. We must have seen in excess of five hundred osprey gliding among the trees, removing the Spanish moss from the trees, and building their nests for the coming season. From strictly a fishing perspective, the other three lakes are more productive but, from the sheer standpoint of beauty and wildlife, you cannot beat Blue Cypress.

F. Texas

Baffin Bay is a bay in south Texas, an inlet of the larger Laguna Madre. It is a huge body of shallow water and easily wadable. It is partially cut off from the ocean so, while there is an abundance of spotted sea trout and redfish, there are no predator sharks.

On two different occasions, I joined my friend from California days, Chuck Cooley, at the Baffin Bay Rod and Gun Club, where he had fished on multiple occasions. The Club was owned by Captain Sally Black and her late husband, Captain Aubrey Black, who tragically passed away in October of 2019. I caught a lot of good-sized sea trout, but asked Aubrey if I could look for a big red (red drum). Aubrey dropped me off along a shoreline with my fly rod. Baffin Bay borders the famous King Ranch and that was the shoreline I was fishing. I had a nine-weight fly rod with a small popper for a fly. As I was walking in ankle-deep water, I saw this wake coming towards me. I cast the popper in front of the wake, and the red hit it hard and fast. I yelled at Aubrey, who was fishing with Chuck several hundred yards away. They arrived just as I landed the fish. Aubrey, who was also a talented writer, wrote a nice little article of how this octogenarian had such a happy day and how Aubrey likewise had a happy day watching the whole scenario play out, see Appendix II. Another great fishing and life experience.

G. California

Most of our friends try to spend some time in Florida during the long and dreary winter days in Pittsburgh. As mentioned, we went in the other direction, spending the better part of twenty winters in Southern California in the desert of the Coachella Valley. We were introduced to the desert when Brian went to law school in San Diego. In addition, our two oldest friends lived in California; Lee and Sheila Asseo in Santa Barbara, and Tip and Judy Davidson in Cathedral City. We ended up renting every year in Mission Hills in Rancho Mirage, located between

Palm Springs and Palm Desert. Mission Hills included five golf courses, each having a number of good-sized ponds often filled with largemouth bass and catfish, to name two. When our grandchildren were young and came to visit, I would set them up with stink bait and they would catch catfish after catfish. When they got older, they would join me in fishing for the bass. We had to be selective on our fishing times since, during normal daylight hours, the courses would be filled with golfers.

My favorite early evening pastime was to fix a tall vodka martini and then head for the closest pond with my drink, my fly rod, and a golf ball retriever. I would then see if I retrieved more golf balls or if I caught more largemouth. A good day would be five or six golf balls and five or six bass. On a couple of occasions, I fished the larger of the ponds (without my ball retriever) and hooked into really large fish. I always forgot my cell phone (with camera) so you only have my word for it.

H. Alaska

I fished Alaska eight times. The first trip was with my old Columbus friend Tip, and a couple of his older friends from Columbus. It was to Bristol Bay Lodge, which today is forty-five years old and is still rated as the best fishing lodge in Alaska. I was in my forties and used to roughing it. This lodge catered to rich old men and their families, and had every amenity from saunas, masseuses, evening movies covering the day's fishing activity, and a five-star restaurant. Tip's friend met that criterion, but Tip and I were a little out of our element. We went out every day by sea plane or helicopter, and fishing was wonderful. It was a great trip but, realistically, should have been at the end of my fishing career and not the beginning.

The next trip was a mid-life crisis adventure that topped all crazy things I have ever done. I hit fifty years old and, in my mind, needed one more adventure to prove my manhood. I had met a fellow crazy fisherman, Phil Thomas, in Costa Rica a few years earlier. Phil was a dentist from Sandy Lake, Pennsylvania and was a very good outdoorsman. Phil trapped fox for supplemental income and made his own fox lure from mouse urine he collected in a series of cages he had built in his garage.

We decided that we would float a river in Alaska without a guide for six or seven days. Phil had a friend who was a flyway biologist for the Department of the Interior on the Kenai Peninsula. He helped us select a small river that was northwest of Anchorage and which flowed into the larger Mulchatna River. We flew into the Kenai Peninsula, fished one day on the Kenai River, and then borrowed Phil's friend's Volkswagen and headed over to start our adventure. A small sea plane flew us over the river where we were going to raft, and landed on a small lake partway up a mountain. The pilot told us to blow up our raft and work our way over to the river we were to float. He told us that when we came to the Mulchatna River, we should go no further and that is where he would pick us up in six days.

We made it to our little river, which was not so little, as it was roaring with high water. No one had been on that river that year (1987). We started our float, which was hectic to say the least. We could not always control the raft and we would often do full circles before we got the raft under control. There were plenty of overhanging tree limbs and we would have to duck our heads to keep from being swept off the raft.

The first night, we set up our tent and hung our food since we could see huge bear tracks all over the gravel bed where we camped. As we tried to sleep, a heavy rainstorm came off the mountain and blew the fly off the tent, thereby filling the floor of the tent with rainwater. Phil was a heavy smoker and he had several cartons of cigarettes on the tent floor that got soaked. He spent the next five or six days without a smoke, which did not put him in the best mood as he went through unintended nicotine withdrawal. He carried an old military forty-five pistol and I carried a 357-magnum Clint Eastwood-type pistol. These weapons were for bear protection but I thought I needed my weapon to use on Phil if he did not keep blaming me for his nicotine problem.

The second day, we pulled over on a gravel bed and walked upstream a short way to fish for grayling and Arctic char, which were plentiful. Out of the corner of my eye, I saw the wind had shifted and the raft had pulled off the gravel bed and was heading downstream with all our food and belongings. I dropped my fly rod and started chasing the raft down the river. It got caught on some rocks on the other side and I violated all fishing-with-wader rules, namely I headed across the river to get the raft. I had tightened my wader belt, but water still started to fill them. I got to the other side and the raft. Phil caught up with me and I asked him to go back and get my fly rod while I built a fire before hypothermia set in. Phil returned with a grin on his face, holding a partially eaten salmon. Apparently, as I was chasing after the raft, I must have scared a bear, who dropped the salmon. Fortunately, I did not see or hear that bear.

The next few days were difficult, but very enjoyable. Beautiful scenery and wonderful fishing. There was about twenty-five yards of vegetation on each side of the river and nothing but tundra beyond that. We finally arrived at the Mulchatna River and set up our tent to await the plane. Unfortunately, the plane did not come that day as promised. I could tell that there was a weather system between us and Anchorage, so we figured the plane could not fly in bad weather, and that the pilot would come the next day. Phil was not a drinker, but I had a bottle of Yukon Jack that I had been sipping on each night. Phil and I finished off the bottle and then tied it to a tree limb, where we tried without success to hit it with our artillery.

The next day, the plane arrived and took us back to the little airport on the outskirts of Anchorage. We got into the Volkswagen with Phil driving as fast as he could until he found a little convenience store, where he headed for the cigarettes at about the same speed I headed for a six-pack. Later, I woke up on a big jet headed home where Phil said, "You dumb SOB. You passed out from the six-pack and I had to haul your rear end onto the plane."

My fifty-year-old mid-life crisis was over and, as I look back on it, I would not have traded it for anything.

The next five trips to Alaska were to the Ayakulik River on Kodiak Island. This is on the southwest corner of Kodiak Island on the opposite end from the town of Kodiak. It is Alaska's largest island and the

US's second largest island extending about a hundred miles in length. The fishing camp was built by Dennis Harms in 1989. It is rustic and comfortable if you do not mind using an outhouse. To get there, you either fly a small fixed-wing plane from Kodiak into Larsen Bay and then a helicopter into camp or take the helicopter from Kodiak straight to the camp. Both are exciting and breathtaking flights.

The Ayakulik is filled with sockeye and king salmon in the summer and steelhead and cohos in the fall. The riffles are loaded with grayling and I have fished both seasons with alarming success. The river is also loaded with Kodiak brown bears. These bears are larger than the grizzly bear, with the males going from six hundred to fourteen hundred pounds and the females going from four hundred to seven hundred pounds. The Kodiak brown bears are matched in size only by the polar bear.

On one of my early trips, I took my grandson Matt, who had just turned sixteen, his dad Steve, Andy and his dad Bruce, my friend Lou Kushner, and Bill Hill and his son David. The first day on the stream full of bears, Matt stood so close to me that he might as well have climbed into my waders. By the end of the week, he was not worried about the bears and was fishing on his own as well as helping the guides clean the fish and do other chores.

On another trip of fathers and sons, my friend Jack Demos and his son Greg and his son-in-law Rob Kruljack joined us, along with Jeffrey and Jamie Shallenberger. Their dad John, my oldest fishing buddy, had fallen off a ladder painting his house, and could not join us. Brian was there as well. The camp had a couple of guides who we had gotten to know quite well. Amy was a talented artist who would take me and my five weight Winston fly rod and fish the riffles for grayling which, at one pound, were as much fun to catch as the thirty-pound Kings. She would also guide my old buddy Bill and me and help us both cross the river which, at spots, was more than we could handle. The other guide, Jake, was as crazy as Amy was sane. He took the young boys some three miles into the North Atlantic in a small Zodiac rubber raft with a fifteen-horsepower motor. They caught a one-hundred-eighty-three-pound halibut. Because of a large shark population, Jake shot the halibut several times with a nine-millimeter Glock and the boys then stood on one side of the raft and hauled the fish on board. The young eighteen-year-old cook from a farm in Wisconsin cut a piece of the halibut into strips and interlaced the strips with strips of the red sockeye salmon. The result was a platter that looked exactly like a checkerboard, which she then baked and it was delicious.

After the old guys went to bed, the young guys played poker and drank beer. One night on a dare, Rob Kruljack took off at eleven o'clock at night and climbed the small mountain outside the camp to spend the night sleeping among the bears. The next morning, Jack was furious and he and his son Greg had to climb the mountain to find Rob, which they did succeed. On the way down, they encountered several bears and it was not an enjoyable experience.

My last trip to Alaska was to a camp on Lake Iliamna called Cusack's Alaska Lodge. I found this camp in a very strange way. I usually went to California for a week or so before Sue joined me and hiked and played golf on my own. After one such long hike, I jumped into the hot tub located at the neighborhood pool. It was normally empty of people early in January, but this time there was another old guy in the tub. We started chatting and he told me his name was Bob Cusack and he owned a fishing camp in Alaska. I immediately invited him to my house that evening and we had a few drinks and discussed fishing in Alaska. He assured me he could accommodate my family, so I signed up. This trip included Brian, Andy, his two sons Will and Ben, and his dad Bruce. They were all travelling from the south out of Charlotte, North Carolina. I was to meet them in Anchorage, where we were to fly to the town of Iliamna to be picked up by Bob in one of his float planes. Unfortunately, my flight from Pittsburgh was canceled and I finally arrived in Anchorage a day late. I made my way to Iliamna the next day, where I was picked up by Bob in his favorite plane, an old antique plane of unknown origin. It was small and had no second seat. I had to sit behind Bob on an empty beer keg and hold on for dear life. Fortunately, there was a thin plastic canopy over the cockpit, but I still felt like Charles Lindberg on his maiden voyage.

Every day, we broke up into two groups and fished different areas after Bob would drop us off with a guide in his more conventional sea plane.

One of the rivers we fished was the famous Copper River. I was fishing with Brian and the guide, and we hung up in some shallow riffles. The guide told us to start walking downstream and he would get the boat off the rocks and catch up with us. I was about twenty or thirty yards ahead of Brian. I crossed a little feeder stream and noticed there was a small school of sockeye where the little stream fed into the Copper. I then heard this loud thrashing noise. A huge bear had run down the stream into the river to catch the salmon. Unfortunately, Brian had just started across that stream and the bear ran so close to him that Brian could smell the bear's bad breath. We were happy to get out of there in one piece.

Alaska remains my favorite place to fish and maybe, just maybe, I will get there one more time.

I. Canada

I have already covered my youth and the several fishing trips I made to Canada with my dad. While working in the steel mill, I flew into Red Lake, which is north of Rainy Lake in Western Ontario. Three of my buddies and I were the only ones on the lake and our short-wave radar and refrigerator did not work, but we made the most of it and had a good time.

In 1970 or 1971, my buds and I traveled to Lake Mistassini through Frontiers. Lake Mistassimi is located three hundred fifty miles northeast of Montreal and is loaded with lake trout, speckled (brook) trout, big northern pike, and walleyes. There used to be three camps there and we went to Vieux Ponte, which is on an island in Mistassini. The speckled trout fishing is some of Quebec's best, being distributed in the lake and rivers and tributary streams that fed into its big lake.

I was still in my early thirties when I started going there, so travel cost was always a concern. Tip and Keith (both from Columbus) and Denny Slevin and I (both from Pittsburgh) decided to drive as far as we could before taking a plane to the island. Big mistake. We had to drive into Northern Quebec, which was not so bad, but the road to Roberval and then onto Chibougamau was dirt and had not been graded yet that year. We had Tip's new station wagon filled with gear and beer, so we were riding close to the road. Tip later found out that we had destroyed the bottom of his new car much like putting a piece of metal into a shot-peening machine.

The fishing was great and we were rewarded with a forty-eight-inch, thirty-pound northern pike I caught and a twenty-six-and-a-half-pound lake trout Tip caught. My pike, which hangs on the wall of my man cave, was the largest pike caught anywhere that year as reported by Field and Stream.

The second year, we drove just to Roberval and flew in from there. It was a long drive and we needed to spend the night along the way. We made it well north of Montreal before we started looking for a motel. We came across an old bar in the boondocks that was very lively and that had a sign that advertised rooms for two dollars. We stopped. It was a Friday night and the lumberjacks had just gotten paid. They were all very thin looking, hard workers who were mostly accompanied by their heavyset wives. We checked the room and it was the worst room we had ever seen. The bed was horrible so we flipped a coin, with the two winners choosing the floor and the losers getting the bed. We went into the bar for a well-earned beer. There was an accordion player who unfortunately knew only one song, "Peg of My Heart." The accordion had a hole in the bellows so along with playing the one song, we got the wheeze every time he collapsed the bellows. After a while, three of us went to the room leaving Denny, who has a Master's Degree in sociology from MIT and a Doctorate from Stanford, to chat with the locals. Denny came up later and I shoved the dresser against the door for safekeeping. Late into the night, we heard gun shots and shortly thereafter, there was a knock on the door. A Canadian Mounted Police Officer said one of the lumberjacks' wives had started shooting at her husband, so they were in the process of arresting the wife. The husband told the Mounty that there was an American upstairs who said he would take the lumberjack home. I am sure Denny had made that offer but I respectfully declined.

The third year at Mistassimi was also quite eventful. We had the sense to fly into Roberval and then into Chibougamau where we got to the island camp by Beaver aircraft. Unfortunately, there was a huge forest fire on the mainland and we sat and watched the explosions as the fire moved from tree to tree through the forestland. Denny and Keith were able to catch a plane out to Roberval, but Tip and I were left stranded another day on the Island. Under Canadian law, all Canadian citizens were required to leave their jobs if called upon to fight forest fires. The result was all our guides had to leave. The plane that Denny and Keith flew in had brought in a couple of new Americans. The camp owner knew I was getting comfortable with the lake and asked if I would guide the newcomers in the absence of guides. After a few days without shaving, I looked more like an Indian than the Indians. I agreed to guide on one condition, namely that he not tell the fishermen I was an American. The owner agreed and I spent the morning grunting and not saying much to the newcomers. Finally, after listening to their BS, I broke down and told them I was just a stranded fisherman. They got a big kick out of it.

The fourth year was completely different. I had befriended our guide Charlie Isserheff, whose dad was German and whose mother was an Ojibwe Indian. Charlie had agreed the year before to take us on a weeklong river trip living in the bush. I knew this would be rough but Denny and I readily agreed to it.

We set out on one of the rivers with all our gear including a large tarp, which Charlie made into a teepee every night for sleeping accommodations. There were parts of the river that we could not navigate so we would abandon the boat and portage the area of the impediment until we got to the next navigable water where Charlie had previously left another boat.

I remember that on each portage, Charlie would place the folded teepee on his back and then place the motor on top of the teepee. I offered to carry that load on one portage but as Charlie placed everything on my back including the motor, my knees started to buckle and Charlie had to again carry the load.

On one occasion, Charlie saw a small bear in a tree and ran the boat ashore and started shaking the tree. Denny had jumped out of the boat and was chasing Charlie. The boat was now going downstream backward until I could start the engine and return to pick up my crazy river mates.

Lots of great fishing including many good-sized speckled trout and walleyes. A trip to always remember.

A second father-son adventure took place in Canada. All the usual suspects from the previous father-son outing were involved. Denny somehow got his hands on a huge RV. We all piled in and headed for the Kawartha Lakes in Canada. The Kawarthas are a chain of lakes in south central Ontario. We stayed at one of the lakes and each parent had a rental boat. The only rule was you could not fish with your own son. Buzzy's son Scottie was a die-hard fisherman even at a young age, so he fished with me. Brian fished with Tip and loved it. He was the youngest and Tip let him drive the boat which, of course, was against the rules. We splurged and one day Scottie and I flew into another lake that was loaded with smallmouth. We caught our fair share and Scottie, now a grown adult, still remembers that trip in detail. The drive home was tiring and we all had to take turns driving the RV. A trip well worth taking.

J. Bahamas

I fished Andros Island Bonefish Club three times. The Club was started in 1988. It was owned and operated by Captain Rupert Leadon for over thirty-five years until his passing in 2012. He was one of life's great characters, all in a good way. He had over twenty children and many worked at the club in various capacities. It is said that every non-family female had to work their way through his bedroom before getting a permanent job. The most famous of all fly fishermen, Lefty Kreh, wrote a wonderful article identifying the Club as a hidden treasure. At night after dinner, Rupert "played the saw" and sang for the guests. It was an old tradition taught to him by his father.

The dining room was located on a deep channel near the boat dock. There was a large patio extending from the dining room all the way to the channel. At night during dinner, we could hear tarpon moving through the channel. One night, I decided we should catch "one of those tarpon." One of my fishing buddies in attendance was Jack Voytko, an accomplished artist and wood carver. He was interested in duplicating a large bonefish that he had caught that day. Normally, we release all bonefish, but he had saved this one for artistic reasons. After he did his thing, I chopped off the bonefish head and attached it to a treble hook on the stiffest spinning rod we had. I cast the bait into the channel; removed an umbrella from an outdoor table; placed the rod handle into the umbrella slot and pulled the line into the dining room where I set it next to where I was going to eat; and finally placed a whole stack of plates on the line to hold it in place. We then proceeded with our cocktail hour and dinner. Partway through dinner, the stack of plates went flying and the jumping tarpon was on. The tarpon made several jumps and he was a beauty, but he got off. Upon inspecting the tackle, I saw the swivel had broken. I asked Jack, whose rod I was using, where he got the swivel. He said he bought it online from a Taiwanese company. So much for cheap equipment!

On another occasion, Brian joined me at the Andros Bonefish Club. The landing on Andros Island is a bit scary because there is a crashed plane at the end of the runway and you must fly over it before landing. The terminal consists of a small Quonset hut. It is located several miles from the Bonefish Club, so you need transportation to get there. After we landed, we went into the Quonset hut and the only person there said someone from the Club was coming to get us. With that, he unhooked and removed the television and left in his old beat-up pickup truck. About thirty minutes later, no one had showed up. Finally, we heard a "thump thump" and Rupert's brother arrived with a flat tire. We asked him why he did not change the tire and he said that he had a flat tire the day before, so there was no spare. We started down the dirt road toward the club on three tires and a rim. Fortunately, a Jeep came by and we were able to flag it down and catch a ride to the Club.

On one of our fishing days, we were in a quiet bay loaded with bonefish. There was a large shark cruising the bay and every time we hooked a bonefish, the shark got it before we could land and release it. We decided Brian should catch the shark. The guide was not very happy with that because he said he had had a bad experience with a shark while diving and was still afraid of them. Anyway, he went along with our plan. We had just caught a little permit, so we put a treble hook on our Barracuda spinning rod and used the permit as bait. Brian cast it out and the shark, which was bigger than we realized, nailed the permit. Brian managed to reel it in, but at the boat, the shark took off and the spinning rod broke into several pieces. Brian still had the rod handle and reel, so he brought it to the boat a second time. Meanwhile, the guide had climbed up his poling platform and wanted nothing to do with the shark. I found a hatchet in the back of the boat and was getting ready to do battle with this huge shark. Brian said, "Dad, why don't you just cut the line?" I accepted his suggestion, cut the line, and off went the shark. The guide came down from the platform and we were on our way. It pays to have a smart kid!

I also fished Flamingo Bay Rod and Gun Club on Andros Island. It is the only lodge on the west side of Andros. It is a high-end club dating back to the 1920's when it was acquired by the Bethel family. Fishing was good and we had a different guide every day. One day we had Beau Strathman, who talked me into trying the Missouri in Montana where he lives. I took him up on it and have fished with him for years and continue to do so.

Bill Hill and Paul Hindes from Family Tyes and I fished out of Acklins Island. We stayed at the home of Bob Bergquest, a guide we had met on the Bighorn and who was setting up winter camp on Acklins. The fishing was good but I had hoped to have a shot at a permit, which did not happen. Ohio State was playing for the NCAA basketball title and somehow I found a bar on the island with a television. The reception was terrible and OSU lost, but it was still an enjoyable time.

We also fished Little Cayman Island, which is one of three islands about a hundred eighty miles northwest of Jamaica. The fishing was a bit disappointing because the guide looked for schools of bonefish and there was a lot of blind casting. We were more used to scouting for big singles or pairs and moving small schools as well as tailing fish.

We did some trolling for Spanish mackerel and King mackerel and blues but, while that was somewhat successful, it was not what we expected. There just was not a lot of options so we quickly crossed it off our list of preferred locations.

K. Mexico

The first fishing trip I took to Mexico was to Cabo San Lucas in the late 1970's. Freddie, Tip, and Keith joined me. We were fishing for roosterfish and other species in the area. We caught a number of roosterfish along with a variety of fish with strange-sounding Spanish names. It was a bit sickening to come in after a day of fishing to see a pier full of dead marlin that had been caught that day. The meat was sold in town but I now understand there is much more catch and release.

In the evening, we would go into town for dinner and on one occasion off to the local cock fights. There was a huge bar with an indoor arena where the cock fighting took place. All the locals would gather around drinking beer and tequila and smoking bad-smelling cigars and cigarettes. Everyone would scream during the cock fights and bets were continually being made and paid off. Freddie bet the fellow next to him and won the bet, but felt so bad the loser became the winner because Freddie gave the money back along with his.

One cock fight in a lifetime is enough.

The best meal I ever had and the worst night I ever spent were all in the same twenty-four hours. The first three or four years I fished Mexico were spent at the Boca Paila Lodge on Ascension Bay, which is a hundred or so miles south of Cancun. This was one of the top lodges being offered through Frontiers.

I had read that Ted Williams had fished Ascension Bay and had caught over one hundred bonefish in one day on a fly rod. I was anxious to find that spot and try my luck. On that particular trip, there were five of us: Freddie, my neighbor and friend Ed Watters, Tip, Keith, and myself.

I was told at the lodge that Ted Williams had caught the bonefish all the way across Ascension Bay at a small group of islands called Três Marias.

Not to be deterred, I asked the camp if we could cross Ascension Bay with guides and a tent and stay on Três Marias to do some serious bonefishing. The camp agreed and Pedro (a head guide) and his brother Georgio led our expedition. My buddy Ed (an ophthalmologist) immediately noticed that Georgio only had one eye, so we headed across Ascension Bay with two boats, one tent, five raring-to-go fishermen, and three eyes leading the way.

Ascension Bay is a large body of water and it took a long time to cross to the other side. When we got there, the two guides sent us off to catch dinner. With Pedro's assistance, we caught a number of small bonefish and chopped them up into small pieces. Using the bonefish pieces as bait, we caught about a dozen beautiful red snappers. We caught a big barracuda as well. Meanwhile, Georgio had captured a bunch of huge stone crabs by sticking his hand down into the stone crab holes. The guides built a small fire to cook the red snapper and stone crabs. They then built a second fire, where they placed the cleaned barracuda wrapped in coconut leaves onto the coals to slowly bake over time.

In the meantime, boys will be boys, so the five us in our early forties drank too much good whiskey chased by a beer or two. The meal was soon ready and it was delicious. Pedro and Georgio had cooked some side dishes like beans and rice as well, so we had stone crab, red snapper, smoked barracuda, and all the other side dishes they prepared. That is the good news.

Now to the bad news. It now came time to sleep. The guides set up the tent on the Três Marias Island we had chosen. Everywhere we looked, there were fiddler crabs and other crustaceans crawling all around. The tent was small and never intended for five people. The guides were smart. They set up their sleeping bags in the two boats. They wanted nothing to do with the horde of land crabs.

We climbed into the tent so crowded that we could not move. Everyone was belching and passing gas and it seemed someone had to take a leak every thirty minutes, which meant that everyone had to wake up to let the person out. When you woke up, your nose was usually in the armpit or worse of one of your bunkmates. Sleeping was a disaster.

The next morning, we got up all the worse for wear, but the bone-fishing was great. We had to leave early enough to get across the bay to the lodge. We were all tired and worn out, but agreed it was one of the best meals we ever had. Ted Williams' record still stands.

The owners of Boca Paila eventually built another fishing lodge in 1988, this one called Casa Blanca. It is located on the private island Punta Pájaros. It is located very near the Três Marias Islands where I had spent that eventful night. I fished there five or six years in a row and was never disappointed. One year, I arrived with my buddy Bill Hill on a Saturday evening. On Sunday, our first day of fishing, I was catching bonefish when I hooked and landed a fair-sized permit, the ultimate fish on a fly rod. With a bonefish and permit in hand, we took off looking for a tarpon, which would make the exclusive grand slam of fishing. Our guide knew where there were some small tarpon hanging out. I was able to hook and land one for my first and only grand slam of fishing. I caught the grand slam on my first day and I had nothing to look forward to the rest of the week except to enjoy one of the greatest fishing spots on the face of the Earth. On another occasion, Bill Hill and I each caught a permit in excess of twenty pounds on the same day. Bill hooked and landed a one-hundred-plus-pound tarpon on a ten-weight flyrod. It only took over two hours to land the fish. The good news is that I managed to get many good shots with my camera during the fight. The bad news is I had no film in the camera. I did not intend to give up my day job.

From time to time, we would see big barracudas while fishing for bonefish. I always brought along a stiff spinning rod and reel and a couple of tube lures. A tube lure is nothing more than a long plastic tube with a treble hook at each end and one in the middle. You cast it out in the vicinity of the barracuda and reel as fast as you can. More often than not, the barracuda chases and hits the tube lure with gusto.

On one occasion, I was fishing with my old fishing buddy John, who had never fished in Mexico before. We were at Casa Blanca. I was in the front of the boat and John was in the middle. I saw this huge barracuda straight ahead of the boat thirty or forty yards out. I quickly put my fly rod down and made a long cast well beyond the barracuda. I started reeling as fast as I could. The barracuda took two shots at the lure and missed both times. The barracuda finally hit the lure, but it was very close to the boat. The fish saw the boat and leaped into the air, sailing forward at a fast clip. It went over my head and John and the guide both ducked in time as the huge fish with two free sets of treble hooks went flying by. It had leaped over the entire length of the boat. Fortunately, no one was hurt and John still tells the story to anyone who will listen.

On another occasion at Casa Blanca, Freddie and I were walking the shoreline after the afternoon fishing and before dinner. We were looking for a big barracuda because Freddie, the orthodontist, wanted a barracuda head so he could put braces on its teeth and hang it in his dental office. We saw this huge barracuda and Freddie hooked it on my spinning rod and reel. Somehow, the line got messed up and Freddie was afraid he was going to lose it. I found a good-sized tree branch on the shore and waded out well above my waist to where the fish was frantically trying to get away. I hit it over the head as hard as I could. The barracuda went belly-up and I dragged it to shore. Freddie made the necessary arrangements at the camp to have the mounted head sent to him. It proudly hung in his office with braces until his retirement.

My last trip to Mexico was to a camp called the Flats of Tierra Maya, located on Chetumal Bay, which is adjacent Belize and near the Belize Barrier Reef. I took my son-in-law Andy, grandsons Ben and Will, and grandson Michael. I took turns fishing with each grandson and had a great time watching them learn to catch bonefish. The last day, I fished by myself and went after the illusive permit. Now is the time

I tell you about the big one that got away. We were fishing between shore and the Belize Barrier Reef. The guide and I both saw a pair of huge permit cruising along. I made a perfect cast with a crab fly right in front of them. One of these took the fly and took off. I had the fish well hooked and he started doing a circle or two around the boat as I was carefully keeping the line pressure on it. The permit then simply cruised away and neither the guide nor I could figure out what happened. Oh, well, the permit of a lifetime got away, but I still fondly remember the hookup and the loss.

L. Central America

In the late 1970's and early 1980's, I fished in Central America five times through Frontiers. Central America was just opening up as a fishing destination and airfares and camp costs were extremely reasonable. I do not think I spent over a thousand dollars for a week of fishing including the transportation.

In Belize, formerly British Honduras, I fished Turneffe Island and El Pescador. In those days, Belize was a very poor country. When we first flew into Belize City, there was a "For Sale" sign on the hospital. We asked the Mexican airline flight attendants where we could go for a beer and something to eat. She told us there was only one place and that was a brothel on the outskirts of town. The food was not too bad. The British had a crew of servicemen on Belize to protect against any incursion by Guatemala, their neighbor. The brothel was full of British servicemen who were being attended to by the Latino girls, so we were left alone for the most part to enjoy our dinner.

Our PhD sociologist Denny had to interview the girls, who took him for many pesos on the basis that they had children in other countries being cared for by their grandmothers.

Turneffe Island Resort is an absolutely beautiful little island off the coast of Belize and adjacent the Belize Barrier Reef. When we were there, it had just been purchased by two young couples from Michigan. They had transformed the camp into a high-end resort for fishing and dining. The fishing was excellent. We knew the young couples who obviously came from money would get bored and sure enough after a year or two they sold the resort.

El Pescador Lodge is on Ambergris Caye in Belize. It is more hotel-like and probably my least favorite Central American destination. Fortunately, with the Belize Barrier Reef, the fishing was good and we enjoyed the many restaurants along Ambergris Caye.

I fished Casa Mar in Costa Rica twice. The first time, Tip was with me. Casa Mar was on the Coronado River, which runs between Costa Rica and Nicaragua. The boats were square-fronted Jon boats intended primarily for river fishing. The guides showed up every morning in one long dugout canoe. Often, they wore baseball shirts and St. Louis hats. Apparently, someone from "Busch Family" (Anheuser-Busch) had outfitted them with uniforms. I asked our guide who they played since we were in the middle of a jungle. He said they play Nicaragua. I asked him how they got there and he said, "You walk to the ocean and turn left." They even had a ball field cut out of the jungle.

We normally fished the river for tarpon and snook. One day, there was an offshore breeze and we were able to get the Jon boats over the surf and into the ocean. I have never had a day of fishing like that. There were tarpon everywhere. Tip and I were busy fishing with spinning rods with artificial mirror lures for bait. We frequently had dual hookups with tarpon jumping everywhere and Tip and I exchanging rods to avoid snagging lines with each other.

For the week, I had fifty-two tarpon hookups and landed thirteen fish. I was second in camp. A fly-fishing guide from Oregon had seventy hookups for the week.

The second time, I went to Casa Mar with a small group from Frontiers headed by Roger Latham, the then-editor of Field and Stream magazine. I had transitioned to salt water fly fishing so I had purchased my first and only inexpensive fly rod and reel. One day, I fished with Roger in the river and had a huge hookup. Roger told me to strip set the hook after the fish had leaped. I was so excited my strip set went all wrong. Instead of pulling the fly line straight back to reset the hook, I pulled the line at ninety degrees to the rod. That fly line actually broke in two and away went the tarpon. Roger said he had never seen anyone break a fly line setting the hook. Again, so much for cheap equipment.

For the week with a fly rod, I had seven hookups and one catch and release. I still had a long way to go in the art of saltwater fly fishing.

The week I fished Casa Mar, Jacques Cousteau's son was there with his entire filming crew to capture the porpoises coming up the river for the snook. The crew could not have been friendlier and we had a wonderful week listening to Jacques Cousteau stories.

The week at Club Pacifico was one of the best fishing trips I have ever taken. This trip included Tip, Don Lampus, Freddie, and me.

Club Pacifico (no longer in business) was located on the Isla de Coiba off the coast of Panama. It is a heavily forested island. At one end of the island is the Panamanian Federal Prison and on the other end was the Club Pacifico separated only by dense forest. A number of the camp staff were prisoners who had earned being a trustee by their good behavior. In Panama in those days, any simple drug offender often ended up in the penitentiary.

We spent the first night in Panama City doing all the tourist stuff at the Panama Canal. That night, we went to the casino, but I left the blackjack table after I had twenty and the dealer dealt himself three sevens to take the pot.

The next day, we got in a small airplane and flew to Isle de Coiba, where we landed within the walls of the Penitentiary. The prisoners were scattered all about, many of them making concrete block from crude, homemade block machines. Don, who owns a block-making company, was absolutely mesmerized by their block-making techniques. It was all we could do to get him on the boat to travel to the camp at the other end of the island.

There were six different ocean currents coming together off the coast of this island. There were fish of all kinds, sizes, and shapes where the various currents intersected along the coast. We had good-sized fishing boats. Each day, we had a choice of the area in which we wanted to fish, provided there was a second boat going to the same area for safety purposes. It worked out very well.

Over the course of a week, I caught a large sailfish and a two-hundred-twelve-pound black marlin, along with many other species. Freddie caught a sixty-three-pound Cubera snapper and everyone hooked up with fish we could not land. A fisherman from Chicago caught a two-hundred-thirty-five-pound tuna on reasonably light tackle and he could not get the cramp out of his hands and arms for hours.

There were twenty-two-foot tides so the boat pier was built high off the water to accommodate these large tides. The best fisherperson in camp was a middle-aged woman who was by herself because her husband was off chasing butterflies elsewhere in Central America. One day, we were all standing on the boat pier at low tide discussing the marlin fishing. There was a freshly-caught marlin laying on the beach far below us. This lady said she would see what was inside the marlin and she climbed down a twenty-two-foot ladder, took out her hunting knife, opened up the marlin, and held up everything from its stomach for us to see. Tough gal, and we young men were all impressed. In those days, the marlin meat was either sold on the mainland or given to the natives.

M. Ocean Islands

In 1984, I fished Christmas Island through Frontiers. Christmas Island is a Pacific Ocean atoll around thirteen-hundred miles south of Honolulu. It is part of the Republic of Kiribati. I traveled with buddies Tad. Freddie, and Don. It had only been fished for a year or two by Frontiers. We stayed at an old motel/hotel called Captain Cooks. I understand it has been redone recently and is now the Christmas Island Lodge. There is ninety-three miles of shoreline and bonefishing flats in all directions. We flew from Honolulu on an old aircraft designed for hauling freight and supplies. There were a couple of seats towards the back of the plane for passengers such as us.

The bonefishing was spectacular. You could walk out on any flat and see bonefish in all directions. One day, Tad and I stood back-to-back digging in our heels and creating a mud duplicative of what the bonefish created hunting for crabs. We got attacked from three hundred and sixty degrees. Our casts were under twenty feet and we were laughing so hard we could barely catch and release the bonefish every cast we made.

There were also giant trevally (GT) in the high surf. I had a few homemade wooden muskie plugs made by Phil Thomas. It turned out one cast per plug was all I could get because each lure was destroyed by the GT. I ran out of lures in no time and had no lasting hookups.

The island is perfectly flat and the highest point is about five feet above sea level. The island is full of tree-like bushes no more than five or six feet high and is home to a few species of birds. A curator from a Los Angeles museum was there to study the frigate bird and the fairy tern, which is native to the southwestern Pacific.

He asked for volunteers to stay up all night to help with his study of the frigate bird. He had a full bottle of scotch and a wife in a bikini, so I immediately volunteered. The frigate bird is forty inches long and has a wingspan of ninety inches. This magnificent bird is also known as "the man of war" bird because it chases birds with fish in their mouths and causes them to regurgitate the fish, which they then catch in mid-air. At night, these birds roost in the small bushes. He equipped me with a miner's hat (big light) and showed me how to walk up to the roosting bird and simply grab it around its body, keeping the huge wingspan collapsed against the body. We then looked for previously placed bands before stuffing the bird in a pillowcase and weighing it. If they regurgitated a fish, we identified it if we could before banding the bird and letting it fly away. Release of the bird was like throwing a frisbee. I must have captured two or three dozen birds over the course of the night. The next night, the curator studied the fairy tern, but Don Lampus accompanied him on that study.

In November of 1997, I had a two-week business trip scheduled to the Far East. Brian was joining me so, again through Frontiers, I scheduled a day of fishing on Midway Island in advance of the Asian business trip. Midway Island is a US territory in the North Pacific. Today, it is a national wildlife refuge administered by the U.S. Fish and Wildlife Service. It is famous for the Battle of Midway in World War

II and it was an important Allied victory and the turning point in the Pacific campaign. Upon arriving at Midway, we were shown a short but powerful video of the Battle of Midway. The airfield was on the adjacent island known as Eastern Island. We noted when we arrived, there was only one other fisherman and he was sitting awkwardly at the bar, having wrecked his back fighting a GT and waiting to return to the mainland.

We fished out of a good-sized pontoon boat. Since we were the only ones there, the two captains on the island both went with us. We trolled with small feathers and caught a large quantity of small fish that were chopped up and placed into chum bags. We anchored off a reef and the captains started to toss out the chum. Fish of all sizes and shapes, by the hundreds, came to the boat for the chum. We each held a big twelve-weight fly rod with a huge red feather fly for bait. The idea was to watch for the GT, who are usually near the bottom. The GT would come up for the chum and the other fish with its mouth wide open. You then made a short cast and hung on if the GT took it. When the GT strikes, it heads back into the deep and into a hole where it lives. If you cannot keep it from getting to the hole, you are in for a long day. After a couple of fights, in which Brian managed to land a GT and a huge amberjack, we noticed that the hundreds of fish surrounding the boat were gone. We looked up and saw a huge fin coming right at the boat. It was a tiger shark, who looked to us to be as long as the boat. The shark grabbed on to one of the motor mounts and started shaking the boat. I was hanging on to a side rail and looked at the two captains, one from Australia and the other from New Zealand. All I saw was fear in their eyes. After a short time, the tiger shark let go of the boat and swam away. I later read in a National Geographic article on tiger sharks that they are known to attack the shiny motor mounts. I can attest to the accuracy of that statement.

Our stay at Midway was short, but eventful, and will go down as one of my favorite stories.

The single best fishing trip I ever took was to the Seychelles in the summer of 2014. Brian's father-in-law, Tom Haney, joined me. The

Seychelles are an archipelagic state consisting of one hundred fifteen islands in the Indian ocean eight hundred miles off the coast of Africa. It is a bear to get to, and you realistically must allow two days' travel at either end. We stayed at an accommodation called Alphonse Island Resort on Alphonse Island. It is an old coconut farm with coconut trees everywhere, a main lodge on one end of the island, and individual A-frame units (one per person) located several hundred yards away. The airstrip and boat dock are on the other end of the island. The first thing they give you when you arrive is a bicycle, which is needed because of the distances between the various relevant locations. One needs to be extremely careful because the pathways are cluttered with coconuts, coconut tree fronds, and large land tortoises that slowly cruise around the island. It becomes even more challenging at night after a cocktail or two and nothing but a flashlight to find your way.

The fishing area is an atoll a mile or so offshore. The top of the atoll is seven miles in diameter. The camp holds about twelve fishermen, and the boats are anchored adjacent the atoll. The fishermen leave together every morning in a larger craft, and then board the fishing boats and go on their merry way. The atoll and surrounding water are home to many different species of fish, many of which I could not identify and which I could not pronounce when told what they were. Each morning was spent fishing for bonefish, the size of which I had never seen before. The guides kept track of your bonefish catches and at dinner, they rang a bell for anyone who caught twenty of those monsters in the morning. The bell rang for me all six days I was there.

As the tides came in, the big fish like the GT came over the edges of the atoll into the center area. These fish were monsters. Hooking them was easier than landing them because in the center of the atoll were thousands of coral heads and the GTs were good at wrapping the line around them.

On one occasion, we were fishing near the edge of the atoll and I saw this huge GT come directly at me. I cast my fly as he approached. He took it and kept going directly under the boat, so I was facing one way with my fly rod, which was bent double down into the water, and the fish was going away from me on the other side of the boat. The guide did a masterful job in getting the boat turned around so I was at least on the same side of the boat as the GT. I fought it for a while but the GT got my line wrapped around a coral head and everything broke off including my fly line.

Later that day, Tom also lost a big GT and his fly line around a coral head. As the two of us walked into the tackle shop with sheepish looks, the proprietor just laughed and pointed to a whole display of new fly lines. Apparently, our experience was a common one.

I never landed a GT, but I did land a forty-pound blue trevally, and that was good enough for me. Between Tom and me, we probably caught twenty different species of fish of all colors and sizes.

We had several opportunities to cast at triggerfish and milkfish, without any success. The milkfish eats vegetation and not bait fish, so the fly looked like a big piece of lettuce.

Everything about the trip was exceptional; I only wish I had fished there earlier in my career because I would have certainly saved my pennies and returned. Two days' travel on either end was a bit much for this old guy.

N. New Zealand

In the mid-1990's, I had to make a business trip to Australia. I could not pass up the opportunity, so I arranged a week in Australia and a week or so in the South Island off New Zealand. Sue and Judy accompanied me. I gave short lectures on US intellectual property law to several IP firms in Australia with whom we had business relationships. One firm left me a note at our hotel asking if I would come to the Marriott to give my presentation since they had asked some their clients to attend. When I got to the Marriott, there were over two hundred people and it was standing room only in their main banquet room. Their clients included a couple of big Sydney universities and the room was filled with college professors as well as other direct clients.

I had some attorneys from my office prepare a PowerPoint presentation. It was above my paygrade, and I figured I could stumble my way through. After all, I was the shoe salesman, not the technician. Luncheon speaker to over two hundred people was another matter. I casually asked the attorney who asked me to speak if I could borrow a young lady to assist with the PowerPoint. It worked out and the presentation went pretty smoothly. They continued to send work to me so I must have passed the test.

After a week in Australia, we caught up with my old fishing buddy Tad and his wife Jean on the South Island of New Zealand. We did the usual tourist stuff for a couple of days and then headed to a great lodge on a secluded lake in the center of the island.

As the five of us sat for dinner on the first night, the maître d' said there was another couple from the United States in residence and asked if we would mind if they joined us? We said no and in walked Beau Schembechler, the head coach of Michigan football and his trophy wife who happened to be from Pittsburgh. Tad was a big Penn State fan and a personal friend of Joe Paterno. I was a Buckeye through and through, and Beau had coached at OSU under Woody Hayes while I was there. We had a wonderful BS session on Big 10 football, the girls all went to bed about halfway through. The next day, Tad and I rented a canoe and fished the lake. We each caught several good-sized brown trout on streamers. That was not our biggest catch. At one point, we looked toward our lodge and saw Beau and his trophy wife take off in a kayak. It did not take long for Beau to fall into the cold water. He held on for dear life as Tad and I came to the rescue and hauled his rear end back to shore. That was our big catch!

Some fishing stories have weird endings and this certainly was one of them.

O. Family Tyes®

In late 1992 or early 1993, I was playing a paddle tennis match between my team, Fox Chapel Racquet Club, and Peters Creek. After the match, the teams always got together for a beer or two, and I happened to overhear Paul Hindes, a Peters Creek player, discussing fishing with his teammates. It did not take long for me to be a part of that conversation.

Paul and Chuck McKinney, both coaches and teachers at Baldwin High School, a suburban high school south of Pittsburgh, had formed a fishing club at Baldwin to give the students an alternative to drugs, alcohol, and other negative influences. The program was very successful but, after a few years, the school was concerned with liability issues stemming from the many field trips the club ran every year. Eventually, the school indicated that the program could not continue. Paul and Chuck were in the process of trying to set up an organization to continue to grow the benefits of the Baldwin fishing club. I became very interested in the concept and agreed to act as the leader of the new, to-be-formed organization. It was understood that I would not participate in the daily activities of the organization, but merely oversee those activities from a business perspective. In 1993, with the help of a lawyer friend and big-time fly fisherman Stan Stein, we set up a 501(c)(3) nonprofit organization under the name Family Tyes®. I was appointed the Chairman of the Board, a position I held for the next twenty-five years.

The Family Tyes® mission statement was, "We at Family Tyes® are committed to youth development and environmental conservation through fly fishing." Chuck was involved in growing the local Family Tyes® chapter at Baldwin High School and Paul was interested in developing school programs and outreach programs throughout the state and further.

Chuck was very successful in growing Family Tyes® at Baldwin High School. The students were involved in fly-tying, rod building, and fly casting. There were also numerous field trips to local fishing waters where the students worked on their fishing skills. I attended a few of Chuck's night classes, where there were over a hundred participants between the ages of eight and eighty. Kids with their parents or grandparents thoroughly enjoyed the experience and the Mission Statement was working. A sixteen-year-old from Mount Lebanon High School built a beautiful ten-weight Sage rod, which they presented to me at one of our banquets. Paul, with the help of Dave Thorne, another teacher and coach from the Baldwin-Whitehall School District, worked to grow the program to other schools and to develop outreach programs. They were successful. In Family Tyes®' heyday, there were thirty-two active programs in schools in Pennsylvania, New York, and New Jersey.

Nonprofits, for the most part, require funding and Family Tyes® was no different. This was my biggest responsibility as Chairman. The fly-fishing industry totally supported Family Tyes® and provided rod blanks for the kids to build their rods, feathers for fly-tying, and other fishing paraphernalia at no- or low-cost prices. By far, the biggest contributor of cash was the King-Mellon Foundation led by Mike Watson until his retirement in July, 2010. Mike was a strong believer in the goals and accomplishments of Family Tyes®. The Grable Foundation and the Hunt Foundation were also significant contributors.

The difference in ideology between Chuck, who wanted to stay small and grow the local programs, and Paul, who wanted to grow the program nationally, became too much and Chuck left the Family Tyes® organization. We then hired Bill Stein as the Executive Director of Family Tyes®. Bill had held similar positions in museums in Pittsburgh and was a capable and sound individual. He did a good job in helping with the fundraising, but the Melon Foundation ultimately cut back on its funding after Mike Watson retired and soon there were insufficient funds to retain an Executive Director. We had to let him go after about five years. The highlight of each year was a fishing trip to Montana. The kids had to pay their own flight. The trip usually included about twelve teenagers from various Family Tyes® organizations and three or four chaperones led by Paul and Dave Thorne. Family Tyes® paid for the vans (normally two crowded vans) and housing was often provided by the local churches, schools, or outfitters. This included the church at Fort Smith, where the Bighorn River runs; the church at Gardiner near the Yellowstone National Park and all its streams; Montana State University; and the Upper Canyon Outfitters.

Another successful program was the national Casting Call in Washington, DC. This was a three-day event hosted by the American Fly Fishing Association in conjunction with the National Fish Habitat Action Plan and the Clean Water Act. Family Tyes® along with Youth

Placement (a safe-haven place for inner city youth at twelve locations in the Pittsburgh area) monitored about twenty kids each year in fly casting and other fishing skills and sent them to Washington to conduct classes for Washington, DC children. The classes were at Fletcher's Cove on the historic C&O Canal that runs through Georgetown. A half day was also spent teaching interested Congressmen and their families, as well as many wounded military veterans from Walter Reed Army Medical Center. The classes were held on the Potomac River. What an experience for the kids, many who had never been outside of Pittsburgh. Casting Calls lasted five years and Family Tyes® and its team of young mentors attended each year.

Like so many nonprofits with funding draining away, Family Tyes® could not exist as a self-sustaining nonprofit. It merged into the Boy Scouts of America. I lost track after that, but in the twenty-five years of existence, so many boys' and girls' lives were changed for the better. I know that Family Tyes® was a great success.

In closing on Family Tyes®, I remember one banquet we had at the Rivers Club in Downtown Pittsburgh. The kids brought and set up an actual door that they walked through, signifying a representation of the changes in their lives thanks to Family Tyes®. One of the boys stood up and gave a brief talk on how he was hooked on drugs and was headed down the dark side of life when he was introduced to Family Tyes®. With a grandparent as an advocate and Family Tyes® as a role model, he was able to turn his life around before it was too late. There was not a dry eye in the place.

P. Non-fishing Vacations with a Touch of Fishing

My family took many wonderful vacations outside of my fishing trips. Regardless of the location, I always tried to find a day or two to enjoy the outdoors and fish. We did three bigtime sailing trips with a hired captain and another couple. We did the BVI's with the Asseos, the Greek Islands with the Potters, and the Dalmatian Islands also with the Asseos. Each trip was outstanding, but I always managed to fish, even if it only consisted of trolling a line with lures or live bait as we sailed off into the horizon.

We spent a number of years in our younger days visiting the Outer Banks with six or eight other families from Pittsburgh. Every trip, I scheduled a day of fishing with the boys, and we would catch a bunch of black sea bass and cook them up for the whole group.

We also spent four days rafting the Green River towards the Grand Canyon. Our children were nine, twelve, and sixteen, so it was quite an adventure. Before getting on our guided raft, I stopped at a general store and asked the proprietor for assistance since I had a nine-year-old son who loved to fish. He advised that we were below the trout waters of the Upper Green River, but the silty water we were in was full of catfish. He sold me a stink bait, which he said never failed. At every stop, Brian would hook up and catch catfish one after the other. I was going to skin a few for dinner, but Sue and our two daughters and the young female rafting guide all voted against it. The highlight of the four-day trip was the most dangerous white-water rapids on the river. As we approached it, the guide put the three girls up front since they loved the bouncing, and put me and Brian in the back since Brian was the youngest and a tad skeptical about the adventure ahead. As we hit the first rapids, the raft spun one hundred and eighty degrees and Brian and I went over the rapids first, to the chagrin of all. I think I still have the marks on my arm where Brian dug his nails into me as we crossed over one small falls after another.

For our fiftieth wedding anniversary, we took our two older children and their five kids to Costa Rica for a week. It was tremendous. We started out on the Caribbean side. We had a naturalist guide named Luis, who was with us the whole time. On the Caribbean side, we hiked and went white-water rafting and one day we all went deep sea fishing. Will caught a nice sailfish, and Ben landed a black marlin. Quite an adventure for the young boys and their grandfather as well. We then flew to the Pacific side, where we kayaked in a rain forest stream and zip-lined over the top of everything. Luis took the kids out at night to find the famous little red frogs, and spent the days identifying incredible bird life.

Perhaps the most memorable vacation was the trip from Longmeadow, Massachusetts to the Prince Edward Islands in a thirty-two-foot Grumman RV, which we named the Grumman Goose. There were ten of us: Sue and I and our kids aged six, nine, and twelve; Sheila and Lee Asseo and their kids aged five (Kevin), nine (Rebecca), and thirteen (Meg). Collectively, we knew nothing about RV life. The night before we left Longmeadow, Massachusetts, Lee invited all of us to his club for a lobster cookout. We pulled out of the driveway and made one turn when everything in the cabinets fell out since we had not locked the cabinet doors. This was a harbinger of things to come.

Driving the Grumman Goose was like driving a big school bus. Up through Maine and Newfoundland we drove. We were always the last one into the camp, so we got the worst hookups. One day, we stopped for the evening but all our ground beef was frozen. We set it out on a picnic table and sent the kids to a junior playground to play while we set up a couple of lawn chairs and settled down for our evening cocktails. Next thing we know, there was a violent bunch of growling and barking and we saw a pack of wild dogs on the picnic table devouring our dinner. We immediately called Meg, the oldest, over and told her to make the kids peanut butter and jelly sandwiches for their dinner while the adults continued with their cocktail hour.

When we hit Prince Edward Island, everyone had a different idea on where to go and what to do. I had diligently studied our trip beforehand and knew that there was a wonderful fishing village at the far end of the island. I won and we headed there. When we arrived, there was a red dye-like substance that covered the entire beach. When our kids came back from swimming, they were red from head to toe. It took hours to scrub and clean them and their bathing suits. Not to give up, I rented a fishing boat and captain, who took us out to sea. The only adult who did not get seasick was Sue, who had to help the kids bait the hooks and reel in the fish. So much for our fishing adventure.

On the way home, Sue jumped ship and rode with her mom and husband, Uncle Bob, who had traveled along behind us in a small two person RV pickup truck. The rest of us struggled back to Longmeadow. The conclusion was that we spent a lot of money to live as we did, but a good time was had by all.

Chapter X

Twilight Years

During my senior year at Ohio State, I vividly remember a BS session with some of my about-to-graduate, semi-adult seniors. We concluded that reasonable lifetime goals included marrying and having a family, earning fifteen thousand dollars a year, and living to see the century change in the year 2000. So much for those goals!

I worked into my eighty-first year albeit at a slower pace. Since I worked continually from my days as a paper boy at age eleven, I can honestly say I worked for seventy years.

There is an old saying that goes like this. "All work and no play make Johnny a dull boy." My saying is slightly different. "Work hard and play hard and life will treat you right." That is how I have tried to lead my life.

Now that my "working period" is over, I am enjoying my twilight years. I gave away my four shotguns, all my fly-tying equipment, most of my spinning rods and reels, my salt water terminal tackle, and my many boxes full of trout flies of all shapes and sizes. I have retained enough fly-fishing gear to cover my fishing trips to Montana and Utah, and the salt and fresh water gear for Florida. I even sold my favorite car of all time, a 2013 Mercedes-Benz SL 550 convertible because it was too low to the ground and Sue could not get in it, while I could get in but then could not get out. Not a tough decision, but a sad one nevertheless.

I try to play golf a few times per week; play bridge three or four days, and do my gardening, walking, and yoga. Apart from bridge, all the other activities wear me out. I also remain an avid reader and only watch television for sporting events.

I have battled and won hyperthyroidectomy, prostate cancer, multiple pacemakers, and open-heart surgery to repair an aortic valve and repair a mitral valve, two hernias, cataract surgery, and a few other medical things along the way. My alleged thirty-minute minor surgery to repair a "minor throat pouch (Zenker's Diverticulum)" turned into a two-week ordeal with tubes down my throat for feeding when the doctor accidentally clipped my esophagus.

None of the above has stopped me from "charging." Life has been good and I will enjoy it to the very end.

Appendix I

A letter Russ wrote to the local newspaper, the Geneva Free Press, on April 2, 1952.

Your Furniture House
Geneva, Ohio
April 2nd, 1952

Dear Folks:

My name is Russell Orkin. That's me in the picture. I'm the feller that dusts, **polishes**, runs errands, sweeps, mops, washes windows, unpacks, lights lamps, burns trash etc. out at "Your" Furniture House. Mr. Spencer says I'm the "custodian-in-charge-of-internal-affairs," and that he couldn't get along without me and maybe he'll get me a uniform on acount of I'd look more official or something and I hope he does.

I want to say right now that if you really want to know about furniture, you just want to take a dust rag and dust it. I get a worm's eye view, kinda. F'instance when I get way down on my hands and knees and polish a chest or a desk I can tell if the people who made 'em did a good job of finishing 'em way back and in under.

They've got real good furniture out at Your Furniture House and most of it's too heavy for me to lift. Donnie (that's the black haired feller that sells) says the reason it's heavy is because it's solid maple, oak, mahogany, or cause it's made in Jamestown or Grand Rapids. He says furniture should be heavy. I like to dust Kling solid maple furniture and Sprague and Carleton stuff cause it's so smooth and easy to do.

I counted 317 lamps we just got in and notice that they have one I'd like to take home to Mom for only $4.95.

They just got in some new davenports, too. There's a green one, a red one, a yellow one that they say is gold, and one that looks like a piece of toast done just right. They've got lots of other ones too and one that's real long so if you want to lay down on it. My dad could really stretch out on it, but he's just got Mom a new Shearman Lawson and it's dark brown with fuzzy stuff all around the cushions that makes Mom wish she had some new tables to go with it, it looks so nice.

If you want to see something that will knock your eyes out, you want to stop in and see the scrumptious breakfast sets that you can't burn the top of with a cigarette for only 79.50. We sold 148 mattresses during February and I had to help get them in and send them out and the breakfast sets too.

I like to work at Your Furniture House 'cause everybody that comes in is so friendly and they tell them that they can bring back anything that they don't like or won't go with the color of the rug etc.

I polish furniture with Guardsman polish they sell for only 1.00 and I like the smell of it and Obie does too. Obie is my dog and he sniffs me with pleasure when I get home after using Guardsman which is the easiest to use and best polish there is that's real good for furniture.

Well, I must close now and get to work — whew, there's lots of furniture out here.

Very truly yours,
Russ

Appendix II

The following column was written by Captain Aubrey Black, co-owner and guide at the Baffin Bay Rod and Gun Club on Baffin Bay, Riviera, Texas.

15 years of guiding and plying the waters of Baffin Bay, I have had many memorable moments. Some were personal, like my 32 1/2", 11 pound best ever trout. Or catching 11 trout over 25", four over 30" on Christmas Day in 2 1/2 hours back in 2008.

While I still love to pursue the larger specimens of our favorite fish, I have found over the years that I receive much more enjoyment through the accomplishments of my clients and friends on the water. Many "firsts" and "personal bests" have happened on board my boat. Each one creates its own story and lasting memory. Father/son moments, time spent with wounded servicemen and women are some that really stand out for me.

Today was one of those lasting memories that will be with me for a long time. Sometimes it just seems like divine providence is involved. None more so than today.

As we stood outside the lodge this morning preparing to pull out of the driveway for the familiar short drive to the ramp, my two clients for the day and I were discussing many things. Among them we were lamenting the fact that Father Time was not very kind. Russ, the octogenarian of the group, said he was still pretty fit and still enjoyed Fly fishing but his eyesight had gotten to the point that he really just couldn't see the fish to cast at anymore.

We splashed the boat and headed out on the bay. The winds were about 12-15 mph and forecast to get significantly stronger throughout the day. I guided the boat along the south shoreline with a couple of places in mind when I started seeing redfish wakes along the shallow grass. Then there were multiple wakes, and then it looked like about twenty wakes bunched together. This looked like a good place to start.

I idled up as close as I could. The morning sunlight with its slightly yellow early spring tinge to it glistened off the ripples the wind created. Those ripples slowly disappeared the closer you got to the shoreline as the trees and bank blocked the wind.

I mentioned to Russ that I thought the redfish might go for a popper of some sort. He searched his gear but had nothing like that. So I dug in my box and found a very little used red/white popper. We tied that on and Russ headed to the shallow water in search of a redfish.

Meanwhile, Chuck and I headed for the grass line where we saw most of the wakes earlier and tried our luck with conventional tackle. The trout were there and hungry so we obliged as much as we could. After about forty-five minutes, our bite slowed down. I decided to get the boat and pick up the two of them and try another spot. Russ was still diligently working the shallows over.

Then, just as I reached the boat, I heard a shout from the shoreline. I was just a few quick steps from the boat so I climbed aboard and pulled out my binoculars and trained them on Russ.............. Bowed Up!!!!

I maneuvered the boat as quickly as I could and as close as I could and arrived just as Russ landed the fish. The grin across that man's face would put the Cheshire Cat to shame. He quickly gave me the play by play of his redfish swimming down the sand toward him pushing up a small wake. A perfect cast and a couple of quick strips to get the fish's attention and Whoosh!! Fish On!! Russ said she made one good long run stripping the line from his fly reel so fast he dared not get his fingers in the way of the handle.

Two more short runs and she finally came to hand. A mixture of emotions flooded over him. Excitement, relief, pride, a sense of accomplishment. I'm really not sure who was more excited. Chuck, me, or Russ. It was such an awesome feeling as I coached him on how to hold the fish for the photo.

Congratulations Russ on your catch. And from what I saw personally today, I don't think it's your last by a long shot.

Milton Keynes UK
Ingram Content Group UK Ltd.
UKHW020319211123
432926UK00008B/289/J

9 798822 921795